Saltwater Fly Fishing
in New Zealand

Saltwater Fly Fishing in New Zealand

Sam Mossman

Copyright © Sam Mossman, 2000
Copyright © David Bateman Ltd, 2000

First published 2000 in New Zealand by David Bateman Ltd,
30 Tarndale Grove, Albany, Auckland, New Zealand

ISBN 1-86953-414-X

This book is copyright. Except for the purpose of fair review, no part may be stored or transmitted in any form or by any means, electronic or mechanical, including recording or storage in any information retrieval systems, without permission in writing from the publisher. No reproduction may be made, whether by photocopying or by any other means, unless a licence has been obtained from the publisher or its agent.

Design John Baanders/Tengate Graphics Ltd
Printed in Hong Kong by Colorcraft Ltd

Contents

Acknowledgements — 6

Introduction — 7

Chapter 1: Beginnings — 9

Chapter 2: Tackle — 15

Chapter 3: Setting up the line and leader — 23

Chapter 4: Casting — 33

Chapter 5: Flies and fly tying — 39

Chapter 6: Fishing to regulation — 47

Chapter 7: Small game — 52

Chapter 8: Catching kahawai — 57

Chapter 9: Targeting trevally — 61

Chapter 10: The challenge of snapper — 67

Chapter 11: Chasing kingfish — 73

Chapter 12: Barracouta and warehou — 79

Chapter 13: The bottom fish — 83

Chapter 14: Deep-water techniques — 88

Chapter 15: The game sharks – makos and blues — 93

Chapter 16: The small tuna — 101

Chapter 17: Yellowfin and mahimahi — 108

Chapter 18: Marlin – the ultimate — 113

Chapter 19: Sweet water and salt — 130

Glossary — 132

Index — 137

Acknowledgements

Most of the photos in this book have come from my own camera, but I would like to thank Mark Kitteridge, Mark Draper, Rick Pollock, Murray Nicholls, Pat Langevad, and Keith Michael for their contributions, and Richard Dobbinson for acting as model for the casting photos.

Skippers who encourage fly fishing are not common, and my thanks go to Rick Pollock, Bruce Martin, Robin Mayo, Mark Harris and Ron Grant, Nigel Merry, Ant Loggie, Alain Jorion, and Mel Sharples who have given me some great fly-rod opportunities over the years.

Top professional fly tier Pat Swift has generously supplied advice, materials and flies that have greatly helped supplement my own knowledge and efforts in fly tying over the last few years.

Anglers Richard Dobbinson, Mark Kitteridge, Rick Wakelin, Carl Angus, Lewy McConnell, Kydd Pollock, Murray Cruickshank, Ross Johnson, and Pat Swift have all accompanied me on various fly-fishing expeditions; and thank you also to all those other fishing mates that have put up with flies whizzing past their ears over the years.

Inspiration and technical advice from American SWF icon Billy Pate, and pioneering Australian fly fishers Rod Harrison and Dean Butler, helped my steps along the path.

Most of the line drawings in this book are from the pen of angling artist John Morgan, with the exception of the marlin teasing sequence which is from Mandy Edwards. My thanks to the IGFA for permission to reproduce their fly-fishing regulations.

Finally, my thanks to *New Zealand Fishing News* for permission to use some previously published material as the basis for some chapters.

Introduction

About twenty-five years ago, I bought a book in a sale in Napier. It was called *The Complete Book of Fly Fishing* and was written by an American called Joe Brooks. Initially, I was most interested in the trout-fishing chapters, but soon started reading the sections on fly fishing at sea. I was fascinated. I was a keen trout fly fisherman, but probably even keener on sea fishing. Here was a technique that combined the two, but didn't seem to be used in New Zealand.

I tied up some of Brooks' 'blonde' patterns, rowed out off Clifton beach in a ten-foot dinghy, and started casting with my old trout rod. My sole catch during that first session was a jack mackerel. It was not much, but it was a start.

None of the US writings mentioned much about the species available in this country. It was all striped bass, tarpon, bonefish and the like. OK, I thought, I would just have to start from scratch and figure it out for myself.

Over the following years, I did just that. Along the way I learned to build rods, convert freshwater fly reels to saltwater use, and tie my own saltwater flies. In those early days there was no specialised saltwater fly-fishing tackle available in New Zealand, and if you wanted to get into saltwater fly fishing, you had to use trout tackle or make your own.

Although I did not know it at the time, I was not alone with my growing obsession. Others were also taking the fly to sea. Starting in 1979, Mike Godfrey set a series of world records for kingfish on fly that still stand at the time of writing. Gary Kemsley and Steve Sneddon tried the fly in northern waters, and some of the 'Rotorua Mafia', including Nigel Wood, Hugh McDowell and Geoff Thomas, prospected Bay of Plenty waters. No doubt there were others too.

Kahawai, blue mackerel, barracouta, and the occasional 'rat' kingfish were the main target fish for me in the early days in Hawke's Bay. Then a move to more northern fishing grounds widened my horizons. After getting severely dealt to by some uncontrollable fish, I began to look for some purpose-built saltwater fly-fishing tackle. Fish like trevally, snapper, albacore, skipjack, and many more made the lengthening hit list.

After finally getting hold of a Fin-Nor #4 fly reel from the USA and a locally made 12-weight rod from Composite Developments, I started taking on some Hawke's Bay mako and blue sharks, ultimately cracking the world record for mako on 6-kg tippet, and hooking myself for life on saltwater fly fishing.

My intent in writing this book is to encourage the development of this exciting form of fishing in local waters by offering information, entertainment and advice, hard won in over a quarter of a century of fishing the fly around our coasts. I hope that the technical sections in the first handful of chapters are not too heavy going, and that the diagrams will help make clear what words sometimes struggle to. I hope to meet you some day out on the salt water, fishing the fly.

Sam Mossman
April 2000

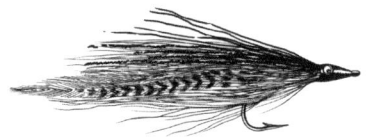

1
Beginnings

Saltwater fly fishing (SWF) is an aspect of angling which has been around for many years. No doubt some early colonial fly fishers took kahawai on trout or salmon fly tackle, probably before the turn of the century. SWF has been a major growth industry internationally over the last few decades, particularly with American and Australian anglers. The real hothouse of development has been in the USA, and much of the developmental work on tackle and technique has been done there. Fishing techniques never seem to explode onto our local scene, but in the last handful of years SWF has finally started to come to the simmer in New Zealand.

This technique has gained an undeserved air as an elitist branch of saltwater fishing, while in reality it is not a difficult technique, particularly if the angler can already cast with a fly rod.

Interestingly, there are probably more converts to SWF from established saltwater anglers taking up the fly rod than there are trout anglers extending their sport from the sweetwater to the sea. There is something about the technique that gets a grip on you, and people seem to take to it with an evangelical zeal, getting more excited about catching a 1-kg snapper on a fly than landing a 5-kg red on conventional tackle.

Once a degree of confidence and competence has been achieved with SWF, there are situations where the fly rod can be just as efficient – and sometimes more so – than more usual techniques with bait and lure. However, overall, the long rod may be considered to be a way of handicapping yourself, and making the capture of a fish more of a challenge, in the same way that a hunter may start to use a bow or even a camera in preference to conventional weapons.

This fits in well with my attitude to fishing – more fun from fewer fish – and SWF is the most fun way to fish that I know. I don't feel a personal need to feed fish to everyone I know, and much prefer fresh fish to frozen, so one or two kept for the table is plenty and a good excuse to fish regularly.

SWF is a compelling form of fishing. Perhaps it is the magnification of the fish's power, as the length of the rod applies extra leverage, making even small fish, like maomao, feel heavy. There are aspects of handlining about SWF – the cast, retrieve, strike, and at least parts of the fight – that are all achieved with your hands directly controlling the line. And that direct contact with the fish is indeed exciting.

The reel also tends to intensify the effect of a fish on the line. Most fly reels are single action, and winding in line can be a slow business, while fish running out line seem to be going further and faster. Even the sound effects of SWF are calculated to get the adrenaline running. The whistling-zipping sound made by dacron backing hauled rapidly over a set of snake guides is music to any angler's ears.

Although fish like kahawai may be taken on fly tackle traditionally used for freshwater work, anglers that become more serious about the sport generally graduate to purpose-designed, or 'crossover', SWF gear, capable of coping with larger, faster fish, and which resists the ravages of saltwater corrosion.

Although quality SWF tackle and flies can now be bought over the counter, there is still a feeling of pioneering about SWF in this country. The area is, if not untrodden, then certainly untrampled. Targeting different species, maybe figuring out a fly pattern and tying it yourself, working out where and how to make the presentation, then actually going out and catching the fish in question ... they are all particularly satisfying.

Finally, there are the fish themselves. As a long-time trout fisherman it pains me to admit this, but kilo-for-kilo the average saltwater fish could tow any trout around backwards. They are generally much faster and more powerful fish than their freshwater counterparts.

I can recall over twenty-five worthwhile species that I have taken on fly over the years. They include kingfish, kahawai, trevally, blue maomao, jack mackerel, snapper, blue mackerel, sweep, john dory, parore, pink maomao, golden snapper, koheru, blue shark, mako shark, albacore, skipjack tuna, barracouta, eagle ray, tarakihi, hapuku, blue cod, trumpeter, mahimahi and large yellow-eye mullet (or herring).

In addition there are a whole bunch of 'wrigglers' that have fallen for the feathers, like spotties, banded wrasse, butterfly perch, piper, scarlet wrasse, spotted stargazer, sea perch (jock stewarts), granddaddy hapuku, goatfish and others.

Other species I know to have been caught on fly rod are porbeagle shark, gurnard, butterfly tuna, yellowfin tuna, warehou, grey mullet, and flounder. Further interesting candidates for the fly rod are species that I have caught on jigs or bait fly strings such as tope and porae, and I am reasonably sure that, with the right approach, blue moki and red cod could also be persuaded to take a fly.

What else? Sea-run salmon are fished with fly in other parts of the world. I imagine that a big, glittery streamer fly worked from a boat off one of the Canterbury river mouths or the Otago harbour in summer would have to work. No doubt someone is already doing it.

The outer realms of fly-rod possibilities include marlin, and I managed to crack this barrier in January of 1998, taking New Zealand's first fly-rod marlin, an 84-kg stripy, on 10-kg tippet from Bay of Islands charter boat *Predator* skippered by Bruce Martin. More New Zealand fly-rod billfish have followed this first capture.

This wide spread of target species, ranging from shallow estuaries to the deep blue offshore waters, gives all anglers a chance to try their hands. The scenarios vary. Estuary channels and banks can be worked with light fly tackle that would be at home in freshwater streams. Using tiny shrimp, crab, worm or even freshwater nymph patterns, mullet, herring, flounder and piper can be caught. I have caught parore on small green rough-tied nymphs.

Early days – the author with some fly-rod victims from Simpson's Rock in the Hauraki Gulf.

From the shore, small streamers will take kahawai, gurnard and trevally. Kingfish may also be encountered, and gurnard, tope, john dory and blue moki are a possibility. On inshore reefs, a mid-water or deeply sunken fly, often fished in a berley trail, may account for species such as snapper, trevally, kahawai, kingfish, tarakihi, maomao, john dory, barracouta, blue cod, trumpeter and jack mackerel.

In deeper water, the difficulty of getting a fly down to bottom-dwelling species increases. Using a weighted fly on a very fast-sinking fly line, I have managed to catch hapuku, blue cod, golden snapper and trumpeter in up to 20 m of water. I am sure that many other species would respond to this technique.

Casting to surface-schooling fish is one of the most exciting forms of SWF, and fly pattern and size vary with the fish being cast to. Candidates include trevally, maomao, kahawai, warehou, kingfish, barracouta, and both blue and jack mackerel.

Finally there are the bluewater fish. Blue, mako, and porbeagle sharks respond to berley trails, and will come right up to the boat to take a fly. Smaller specimens that gamefishermen would scorn on normal tackle can provide a huge amount of fun for the fly rodder. A number of yellowfin tuna have been taken on fly, and I have already mentioned marlin.

Possibly the greatest all-round fun can be had fishing for the common small tuna species: skipjack and albacore. It is hugely exciting to cast to these fish in a 'meatball'

Saltwater fly fishing is the most fun way to fish that I know.

situation, when the fish are on tap, and eager to take your fly. Knowing that a hook-up will be followed by a warp-speed run only adds to the anticipation.

I won't kid you that SWF is more efficient than bait or jigs, but it is a lot of fun, very satisfying, and a chance to try something new. There is a whole world of saltwater fly fishing out there waiting. It is exciting, challenging, and you are only limited by your imagination. It is possible to catch nearly every species of fish on fly.

The first fish

Nothing encourages an angler like success, and for someone trying SWF for the first time it is important to catch some fish – any fish – just to get the feel of the system, and to know that it works, before getting more involved with the technicalities.

Tackle may be a retired trout rig, handed down or cheaply purchased. This sort of tackle has a lot of drawbacks for SWF in the long term but may be pressed into service for initial attempts. If you can't already throw a line, some basic instruction (see Chapter 4) should see you casting 10 or 15 m – enough to get by in many situations.

Don't worry too much about complex leaders at first. They are designed to milk maximum knot strength out of the mono, and this is not so critical when merely trying to get a fish or two under the belt. A straightforward length of 4 or 6-kg line will do the job for many fish. Tie a loop in one end (see surgeon's end loop in Chapter 3) and loop-to-loop it to the end of the fly line. Tie the fly to the other end with an improved clinch or uni knot.

For flies, many freshwater patterns will work in saltwater; smelt patterns, such as the grey ghost, are good. Be aware that bronzed freshwater hooks will rust quickly when exposed to the salt, however. Specialised saltwater flies are usually tied on stainless or heavily plated hooks, and if you do not tie your own (see Chapter 5), they may be purchased from many specialist fishing tackle stores. A couple of common and useful fly patterns are the deceiver and Clouser's minnow. Start with a couple of each in sizes #6 or #4, basic white, or with a red, blue or green overlay.

Initially, it is a good plan to start fishing where you are going to get a lot of shots at fish. The species that most people start with is kahawai. These fish range around most of the country (although they have suffered badly at the hands of purse-seiners in some areas), they will take a fly readily, fight well, but can be handled on the tackle described. You will learn a lot about the realities of SWF in a couple of hours with a school of obliging kahawai.

Kahawai are an ideal fish to start on, and the mainstay of much saltwater fly fishing in New Zealand.

Kahawai can be found near river and harbour mouths in many areas, in surface schools, or can be attracted by berley to rocks or boats anchored near reefs, islands or headlands. Cast your fly out, let it sink a little, then strip it in with half-metre pulls (much faster than a trout retrieve).

You can learn a lot about the basics of SWF in a couple of hours with a school of obliging kahawai.

Jack mackerel are another ideal fish to start on and can be caught regularly on small flies.

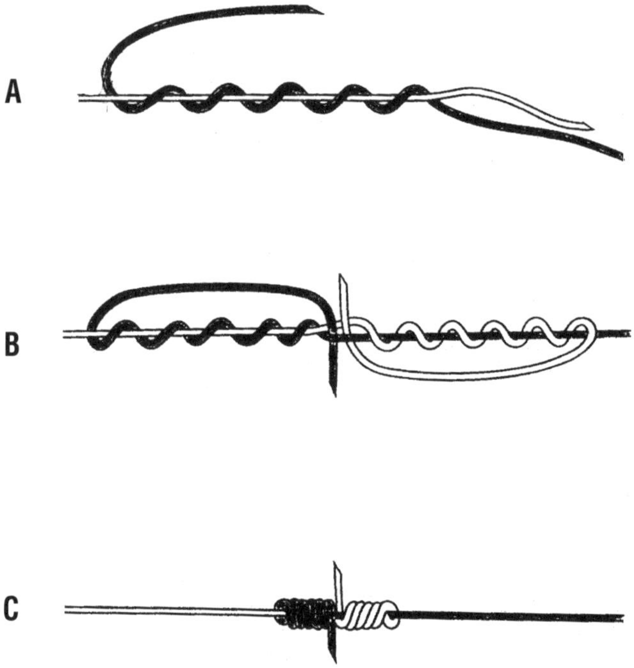

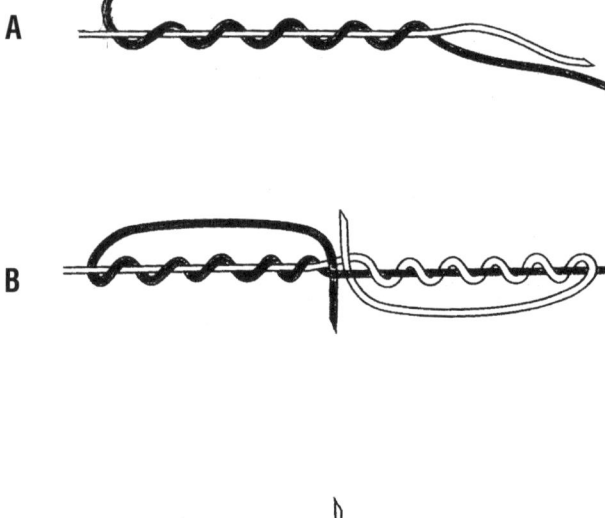

Diagram 1: blood knot

Although trolling the fly behind a boat is not regarded as 'real' fly fishing, it is a successful technique, and a good way to hook a few fish, allowing you to get a feel for the tackle.

Other fish which may readily be available for those starting out are the dreaded barracouta (you will need to add a short length of wire to the end of the leader – see Chapter 12) and jack mackerel.

These small mackerel often feed under lights (such as those found on wharves and bridges) at night, and also respond well to berley. Much smaller flies, such as #10 or #12, are needed to catch these fish. A useful idea is to cut the flies off a sabiki bait fly string and attach one to the end of your leader with a blood knot.

Mackerel are not hard to land, but are good fun, and the occasional kahawai, koheru, or XOS mackerel can make life exciting.

With a fly in the water, you never know what you are going to catch next.

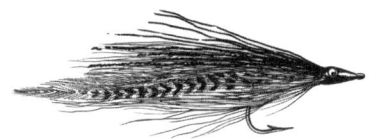

2
Tackle

When I first started dabbling with SWF around twenty-five years ago, there was no purpose-designed equipment available in New Zealand. I started with trout gear, and quickly discovered its shortcomings. While you can get by with medium to heavy trout gear for a number of the smaller species, there are problems with it. One is corrosion: much freshwater tackle is simply not designed to cope with the ravages of salt water.

The gear

If you intend to press the larger sizes of trout tackle into service in the salt, be prepared to fully strip, clean and wash all your gear each time you use it. This includes stripping all the line off the reel, and washing the line and reel, winch fittings, guides and tip. All of this is good practice on dedicated saltwater gear too, but is absolutely essential to stop freshwater tackle from dissolving into blisters of white powder.

I also found that trout reels without counterbalances shook and shuddered like demented hula dancers under the speeds that saltwater fish subjected them to, that fast-moving fixed handles delivered some nasty cracks to slow-moving fingers, and that attempting to slow dacron backing at high speed could result in some impressive cuts and burns.

In addition, I discovered that the extra buoyancy in salt water sand-bagged the sinking action of fly lines, and that the delicate casting actions of trout rods made little impression when trying to lift a determined sea fish from the depths.

Having fallen into most of the traps for young players when I started with SWF, I feel qualified to give this advice: if you want to move beyond dabbling with the odd kahawai and mackerel, get into the right gear. Usefully, there is more and more crossover tackle available these days – tackle with quality fittings and finishes that is suitable for both fresh and saltwater work.

Quality equipment is not cheap. In some instances the price is not far off the cost of gamefishing gear. If you are not willing to spend the money that will buy you top-quality tackle, you will really limit yourself to the middle ground and small to medium-sized fish. This may be fine initially, but as you get a grip on SWF (and it gets a grip on you), you will probably develop an urge for better tackle. As in any field of endeavour, having the right tools for the job makes life a lot easier, and, most importantly, more enjoyable.

Rods

Fly rods are rated by 'line weights'. This is an arbitrary system of numbers, and has no relation to the breaking strain of the line, as with conventional tackle. Fly rod 'weights' relate to the rating of the fly line with which they are designed to be used, creating a balanced casting unit. This relationship is not hard and fast, of course; many anglers prefer to 'over-line' a rod by one or two line weights to make for easier casting in windy conditions, easier short-range casts, and other reasons.

In general, however, a 9 to 10-weight model will cover fish up to medium weight, and the 10–12 weights will take most of the medium to heavy species. For tough sluggers like big kingfish, tuna and sharks, the 12–14 weights are normally used.

This is conventional SWF wisdom, but more fun may be had with lightweight species by dropping to lighter tackle (see Chapter 7), such as a 5-weight rod and 2-kg tippet. A medium-sized kahawai on such gear is a real challenge.

At the other end of the scale, when I first started planning the capture of a New Zealand marlin on SWF, I designed a rod especially for the job. Nominally, it is rated as 14+, and is both shorter and more powerful than normal, with the accent on fighting big fish rather than casting all day. With SWF rods there is a fine line to tread. A delightful casting rod may not have the grunt to lift a deep-plugging fish, and vice versa. A lot of the US market for saltwater fly rods is in shallow-water 'flats' fishing, where casting ability may be more important than the rod's qualities as a fighting stick. Perhaps it is a little the other way here in New Zealand. Some 'flats'-type fishing is available in estuaries

SWF rod actions tend towards more powerful butt actions. Here, Murray Cruickshank works on a 40-kg blue shark.

and beaches, but more fishing is done from boats, and from rocks that drop off quickly into deeper water.

It is fortunate for newcomers to SWF that there is a reasonable amount of SWF gear available these days. In addition to a wide range of imported rods, Kiwi companies Composite Developments (CD Rods) and Kilwell make excellent SWF rods, with saltwater componentry and powerful butt fighting actions. There is probably little point in discussing particular models, as ongoing development will date this information quickly.

When shopping for SWF rods, look for graphite/stainless, or heavily anodised alloy reel seats to cope with the corrosion problem. SWF rods should have thick, extra large-diameter snake guides or ceramics to cope with bulky connecting knots and to avoid 'choking' large-diameter fly lines on the cast. Likewise, the stripping guide and tip should be of a larger size than is usual for freshwater rods.

SWF rod actions are, of necessity, much more powerful in the butt section than freshwater rods. This is needed to lift fish from deeper water, something that is seldom required in fresh water. For this type of work, and to take the knocks of everyday fishing, the blank needs to be robust. Check the wall thickness at the ferrule.

A short extension butt on a fly rod helps keep the reel clear of clothing.

A short extension butt, to keep the reel off the deck and away from your clothing, is useful, and on the larger sizes of rod a fighting fore grip is an advantage with big fish.

Reels

SWF reels usually play a much more important role in playing a saltwater fish than those used in fresh water. Saltwater fish often run further and faster, and this is where a good drag and robust construction become vital. The best reels are machined from a single section of aluminium bar stock, ensuring the strongest construction that will not deform or separate under the pressure of powerful fish and that exerted by very tightly packed line wound on under strain. Aluminium is used for its combination of strength and light weight, but needs to be protected by heavy anodising or other protective finish to avoid corrosion.

Reels intended for light to moderate use may feature one-piece cast spools, which will normally stand up to this sort of work. Many reels designed with freshwater use in mind

For big fish, reels need spools machined from a single block of aluminium. This spool separated after a fight with a good yellowfin.

have the spools assembled in several pieces, but may be used for light saltwater work.

There are two basic types of SWF reel: those with fixed handles (that will spin with the spool as line runs off), and those that have an anti-reverse mechanism that allows the handle to remain stationary while the spool unloads. There are differences of opinion about which is best. Fixed handles are popular with some SWF anglers because of the positive wind characteristics when the drag setting is light – when you wind the handle, you get line – but the anti-reverse is very comforting when playing very fast and powerful fish on the heavier tippet classes. In this case a reasonable drag setting may be used that does not give line-slippage problems when winding the handle.

Personally, I use reels of both types, and tend towards fixed handles on light to medium reels, but anti-reverse for heavy duty. Note that a fixed handle requires a counterbalance on the opposite side of the spool so that the reel spins smoothly when the spool unloads.

Reels designed for SWF fishing are, of necessity, fitted with drag systems that can apply more pressure and operate smoothly at much higher

A mix of SWF reels, including three Fin-Nors, a Hardy, a Sage and an Alvey.

levels than freshwater reels. Some are multi-washer types, while some of the smoothest performances are achieved with large oil-soaked washers of cork composites. A further standard design feature is an exposed spool rim that may be palmed to further supplement the drag.

Spool capacity used to be a major factor in sorting out a reel for SWF. For a start, you needed a big reel to allow enough backing to cope with saltwater fish, although in practice 350 m of usable backing is enough to cope with all but big gamefish. Secondly, nearly every fly reel has a 1:1 retrieve (one turn of the handle means one turn of the spool), therefore the larger the spool, the more line you retrieve per handle turn – important on fast-moving fish. This used to mean that a large-spool reel was packed with a lot of backing that was never used, just to ensure a reasonable rate of retrieve.

With the advent of polyethylene superbraid lines, this has changed. These lines, used as backing, are extremely thin for their breaking strain, and allow big-game capacities on moderate-sized reels. In fact, they have made it necessary to bulk out the spools with a load of dacron first, 'top-shotted' with the superbraid, for reasons of economy (the superbraids are expensive lines, and many reels could take up to 1000 m), and to keep the spool diameter large, so that a maximum amount of line is retrieved per

A pair of Billy Pate reels: (left) a Tarpon model with fixed handle and counterbalance; and (right) a Marlin with anti-reverse handle.

Large-arbour reels, such as this Tibor, are a reflection of the development of superbraid backings.

handle turn. This, in turn, has led to the design of 'large-arbour' spools that make the spooled reel lighter and do away with the need for packing. This new spool design is becoming more popular, and making a dent in more conventional reel design sales.

Purpose-designed SWF reels have always been expensive, and not exactly high-turnover items. This means that often only specialist fishing stores will have any in stock. However, your local tackle store may well get specialist SWF tackle for you if you know what to ask for. There are a number of large freshwater and 'crossover' reels which are saltwater capable, including the largest Youngs and the Scientific Anglers Systems II models.

There is a wide range of purpose-designed SWF reels available today, the bulk of them American made. Some have New Zealand distributors, although these can come and go. Penn International Fly Reels are reliably represented. The Australian-made Alvey SWF reels are robust, dependable, and resistant to corrosion.

Other well-known makes are Fin-Nor, Billy Pate/Tibor, Ross, Hardys, Fenwick and Abel. There are a great many others, many falling into the 'boutique' category. Those that do not have local representation are still available through the wonders of credit cards, mail-order, and the Internet.

When buying a reel, factors to consider are: the size and strength of the fish you intend to pursue (this will dictate the backing capacity and the level of construction, and hence the price of the reel); the line weight you intend to fish; and the rod with which the reel must balance.

As with other types of fishing tackle, a balanced rig is what you should endeavour to achieve.

Lines

One of the definitive differences between fly fishing and casting with conventional tackle is that, with conventional equipment, the lure pulls the line off the reel. With fly casting, it is the weight of the line that carries a light lure out to the fish. The line is the third component of a balanced SWF assembly, and balance is achieved by matching the line 'weight' with the coding marked on the rod. As mentioned earlier, many anglers like to over-line their rods by one or two weights to aid casting, especially in windy conditions; for example, using a 10-weight line on a 9-weight rod. Recently, a number of line manufacturers have started giving line weights in grams rather than the AFTMA (American Fishing Tackle Manufacturers Association) rating system. The following is a rough guide to these systems:

Grams weight	AFTMA equivalent
100	3 – 4
200	5 – 6
300	6 – 7
400	8 – 9
500	10 – 11
600	12 – 13

This is where things start to get complicated. There are a great many different sub-types of fly lines. There are sinking lines and floating lines. There are those that sink fast

At the end of a day's fishing, fly lines should be washed in fresh water to remove dried salt that inhibits casting and causes corrosion.

and those that sink slowly, and a whole range of sink rates in between. There are some that hover in mid-water, and those that sink at the tip and float at the back.

Just to make it more complex, these lines come in a range of different tapers that have different casting characteristics. The old universal coding system of DT = Double Taper, WF = Weight Forward, SH = Shooting Head, and L = Level line has been swamped in a forest of codes used by individual line manufacturers describing just their own products.

Too much information – let's cut to the chase. For the most part, the delicate presentations required for trout fishing are not needed at sea in New Zealand. Of much higher priority are distance and coping with wind. To this end, weight-forward and shooting-head lines are the two most useful types. Both of these lines have the bulk of their weight towards the fly end of the line, making them easier to cast further and in windy conditions.

The weight-forward line is a one-piece line, while the shooting-head line is much shorter and heavier, and has a lighter shooting line attached to it. The heavier shooting head tows out the lighter shooting line when the cast is made. The most useful lines for New Zealand use are either of these types of lines, in a line weight to suit your rod.

The other division of fly lines is sink rate/floating and so on. Depending on the situations in which you fish, differing types of line are more suitable. The extra buoyancy of salt water over fresh, and strong currents, will see those fly lines that would bomb to the bottom in a lake, wafting around in mid-water at sea. If you are trying to fish the bottom, greater depths than in fresh water are often involved. All of this makes the fastest-sinking line you can get one of the most useful.

I am a fan of the Teeny TS Saltwater fly lines, a series of very fast-sinking weight-forward lines with floating back sections. Many other line manufacturers now have their own versions of these lines. The sinking head easily pulls down the floating section, but the line does not sink in a heap and risk tangling on the bottom.

Surface-feeding fish may be moving so fast that a weight-forward or shooting-head line is a necessity. A fast-sinking line of this type can be thrown with minimal false casting, it casts further than a conventional line, maximises line capacity on the reel, and it gets under the surface quickly when it hits the water.

A second type of line that is very useful is a weight-forward intermediate-sinking line. Such a line is very useful for fishing shallow estuaries, beaches in calm conditions, and when working surface-feeding schools of fish such as trevally, mackerel and kahawai.

There are occasions when other types of line may be useful, but the two types mentioned will cover most situations, most of the time, with the deep-sinking line probably more useful.

Leader material

While any monofilament can be used to make a tippet (leader or trace) for knock-about fly fishing, there are several things to take into account. First, if you intend to fish to IGFA regulations (see Chapter 6), your leader must break at or below its stated line weight when tested. Most monofilaments that fall into this group will be marked as such on the spool – 'IGFA class' or similar.

Secondly, because of the limitations on the length of the protective shock tippet (30 cm – see Chapter 3), the class tippet may have to endure considerable wear in the course of a fight with a big fish. This has led to the development of a number of very hard-wearing specialist SWF leader materials. These are often a relatively large diameter for their breaking strain, and have a hard springy feel to them. This type of mono often does not have great knot strength, so care must be taken with leader construction. I have had excellent results on big fish, including sharks, since using this type of leader.

Three brands favoured for this type of work are: Platypus Alloy, Mason Hard Line, and Stren High Impact Hard Mono Leader. None of these is particularly easy to get hold of, but all of these lines have New Zealand agents.

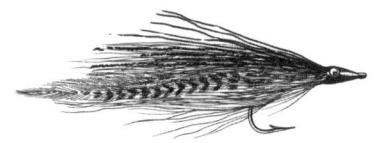

3
Setting up the line and leader

A big albacore hit my slowly sinking fly deep under the boat and, as the hook went home, took off in a panic-stricken run, taking me deep into the backing before settling into a deep-plugging fight. While slowly working the fish back, I mentally added up the knots and other connections in the line that the fish and I had between us – thirteen! – each one a potential weak point. As I slowly regained each connection, I was grateful that it had held up and allowed us finally to boat the fish, a national record of 10.4 kg.

The best captures are often made because a large number of things fail to go wrong! Thirteen or so connections may seem like an awfully complex line and leader system, but if it is done correctly, it gives maximum strength.

As usual with fishing, there are many different ways to do anything, but what we are trying to achieve are strong connections with a small, smooth profile that will run easily through the guides. In addition, we want the convenience of two points where we can easily change the fly line and the leader.

Prevention is better than a cure

There is one thing well worth doing for the long-term protection of a fly reel before first winding on any line: add a protective coating to the spool and the inside surfaces. Salt will accumulate deep down under the line load and attack the inside surfaces of the reel, regardless of how carefully you wash and clean it. A very thin smear of Vaseline or wax car polish will form a barrier that stops the salt attacking the finish of the reel. Re-apply this protective coating each time you strip and clean the reel.

Packing

As mentioned in the previous chapter, with the advent of fine-diameter superbraid backing lines, it may be necessary to pack the reel (depending on whether it has a large or small arbour) with some form of line to bring the backing and fly line to a large diameter, creating advantages in line retrieve speed.

You can do this with any old string (although preferably something that will not soak up and hold a lot of water). Your backing does not necessarily need to be tied to it. I prefer to use dacron, which I attach to the spectra backing by tying a Bimini twist in the spectra and using the resultant double line to tie a double uni knot with the dacron packing. This allows the packing to be used as reserve backing – you never know when you may need a little more line.

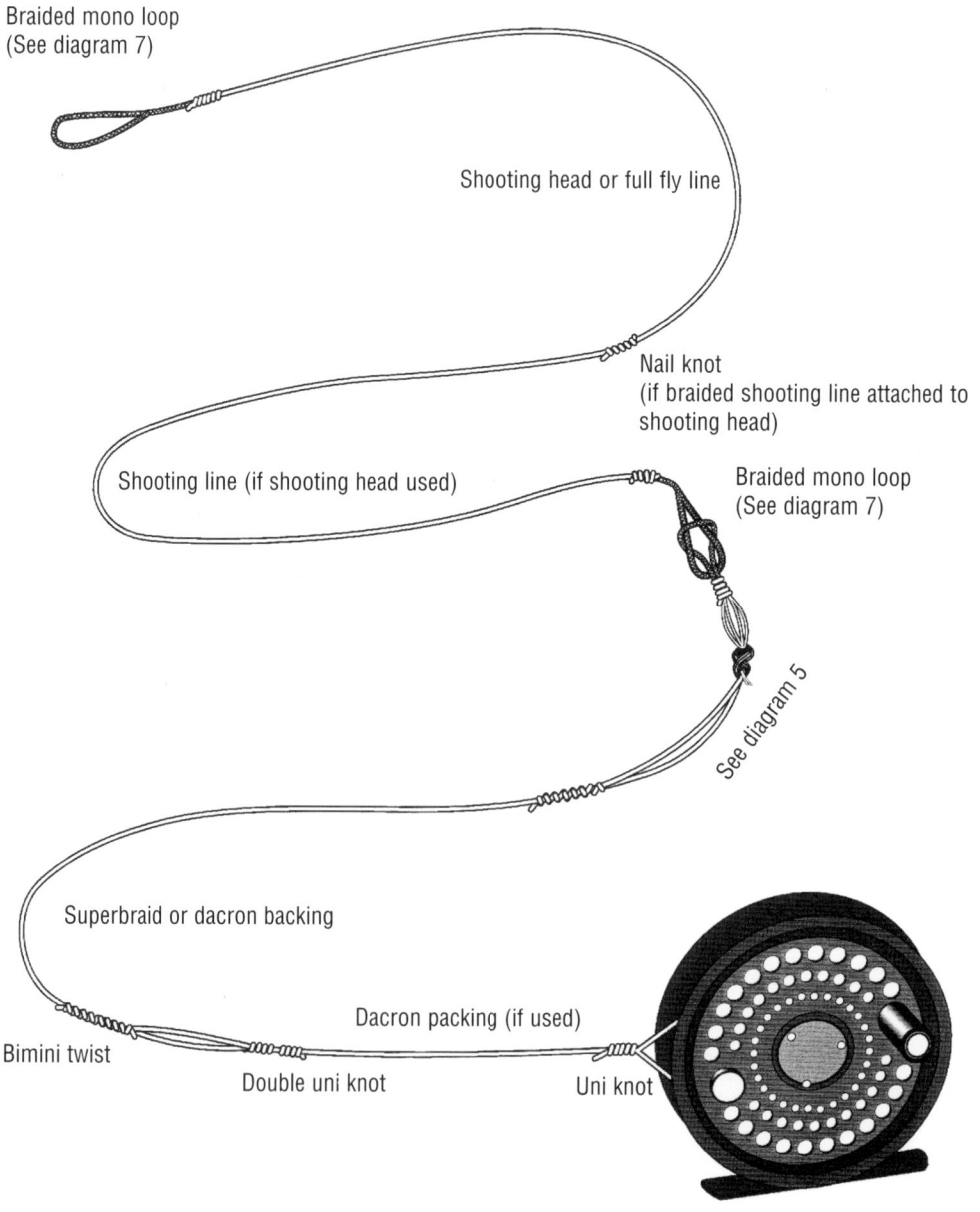

Diagram 1: Reel to fly line assembly

Setting up the line and leader

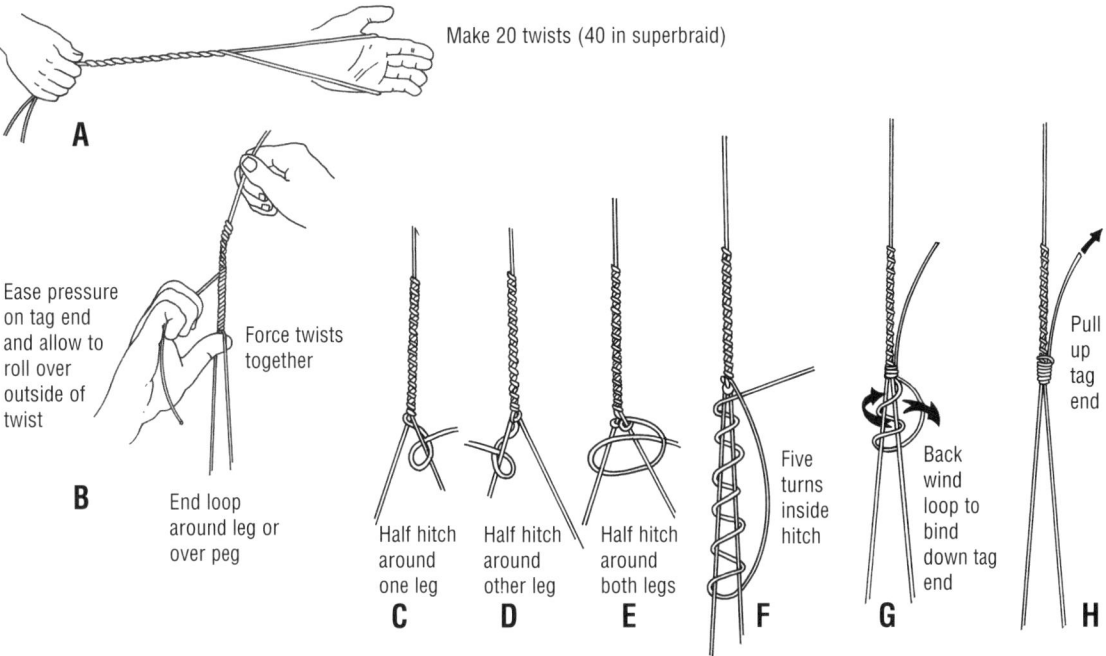

Diagram 2: Bimini twist

Backing

Either the packing or the backing (if packing is not required) is attached to the reel arbour with a uni knot. It is well worth having a strong knot at this point. I have been taken to the spool knot a number of times by fish, but still brought them back. There is a lot of stretch in the system when all the line is out, which can save the day. At worst, as long as you have a good spool knot, your line should snap at the leader, and you will save your expensive fly line and backing (and, incidentally, save the fish from sure death if it is left towing all that line around).

Favoured backing materials are dacron or superbraid (either spectra or micro-dyneema). Dacron is fine for knock-around fishing and still performs well. Superbraids have the advantage of being thinner and so increase spool capacity while reducing the drag created

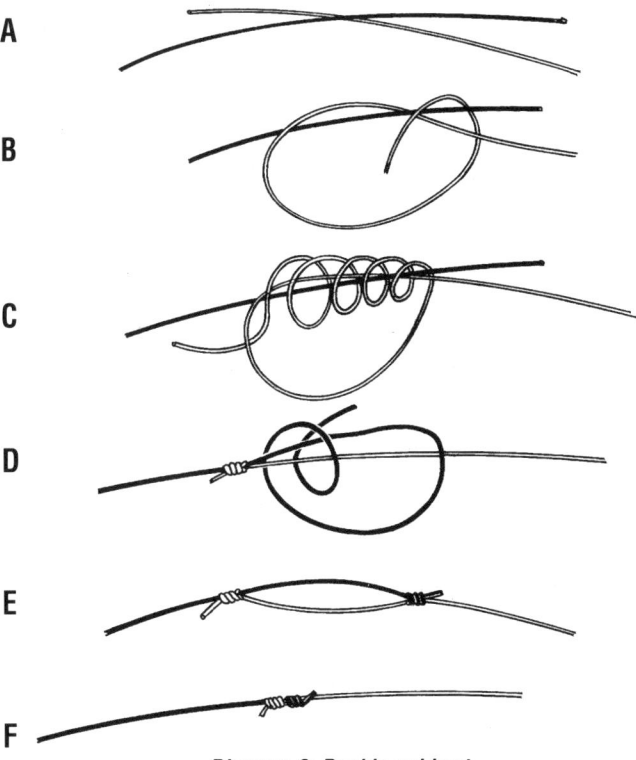

Diagram 3: Double uni knot

25

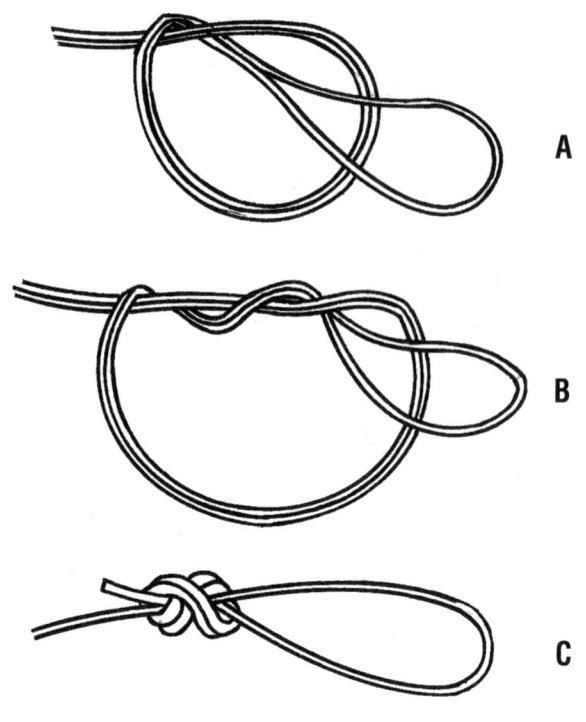

Diagram 4: Figure eight or surgeons end loop

by a fish towing the backing through the water. The line to get is the limper braid, as distinguished from the cheaper 'fusion' construction, which is a lot more wiry.

On the down side, the superbraids are more expensive, and are a bit harder on the hands (I use a glove when playing big fish). When winding superbraid backing onto the reel, wind it on as tightly as possible. Because it is so fine in diameter, it will cut into itself under pressure if it is not wound on tightly, then 'bury' and jam up, causing a possible bust off.

Superbraids also need more complex knots to keep the line strength up. If tying a uni knot in superbraid, first double the line over and tie the knot in two thicknesses, and make ten turns in the line rather than the usual six.

The backing is pretty much a permanent fixture on the reel, but fly lines may be switched around more regularly. Consequently, it is a good idea to put a large loop in the end of the backing; this can be used to attach and detach fly lines in a loop-to-loop fashion. The loop needs to be large enough to pass the fly reel through, so that you do not need to pull the whole fly line through when attaching or detaching. This loop can be made with a figure eight loop or Bimini twist in dacron.

In superbraid it is a much more complex task getting a strong connection. Make a Bimini twist (with forty turns rather than the usual twenty), then double the doubled section with a figure eight loop, so that there are two thicknesses of line on each side of the double. This will help boost the diameter of the superbraid and help prevent it from cutting through the loop to which it is attached.

If there is still a considerable difference in the diameters of the loops that are being joined, something further may need to be done to even them up and to avoid the

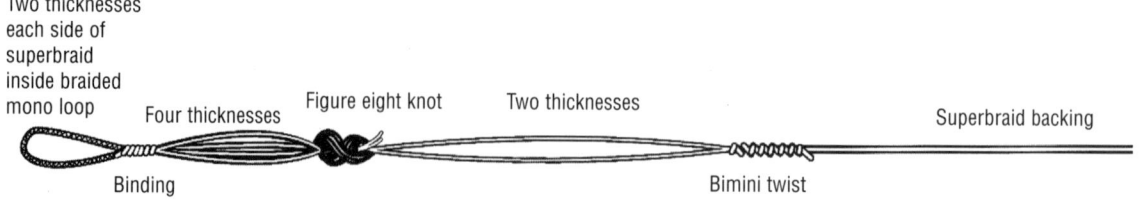

Diagram 5: End loop in superbraid backing

thin one cutting into the thick one under pressure.

My answer to this is: after making the Bimini twist, but before making the figure eight knot, take a length of braided mono (this is a hollow-centred line made of fine monofilament in a circular braid) and pull the superbraid loop through the centre of the braided mono using a doubled-over section of fine wire (15 to 20-kg single-strand trace wire is good).

Now the figure eight knot can be made so the braided mono is captured in the loop that is formed. The two ends of the braided mono are bound down with fly-tying thread or similar, then the whole assembly is coated with a product called Aquaseal, initially made for repairing waders. This bonds the whole assembly together but remains flexible, and smoothes out the lumps and bumps when they run through the rod guides.

This all sounds pretty complex, but done once and well it is unlikely that it will need to be done again for a long time.

Fly line/shooting line

The fly line (or shooting line if you are using a shooting-head system) should be joined to the backing with a loop-to-loop system so that lines can easily be changed. We have just made the loop on the end of the backing, so we now need a loop on the end of the fly line or shooting line.

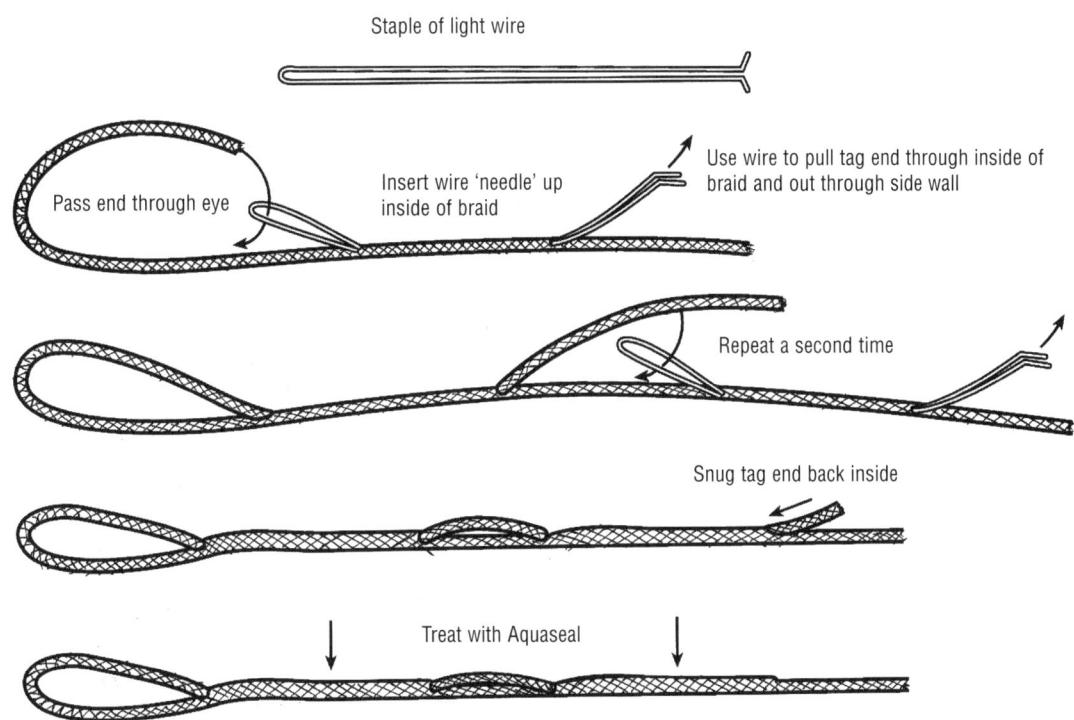

Diagram 6: End loop in braided shooting line

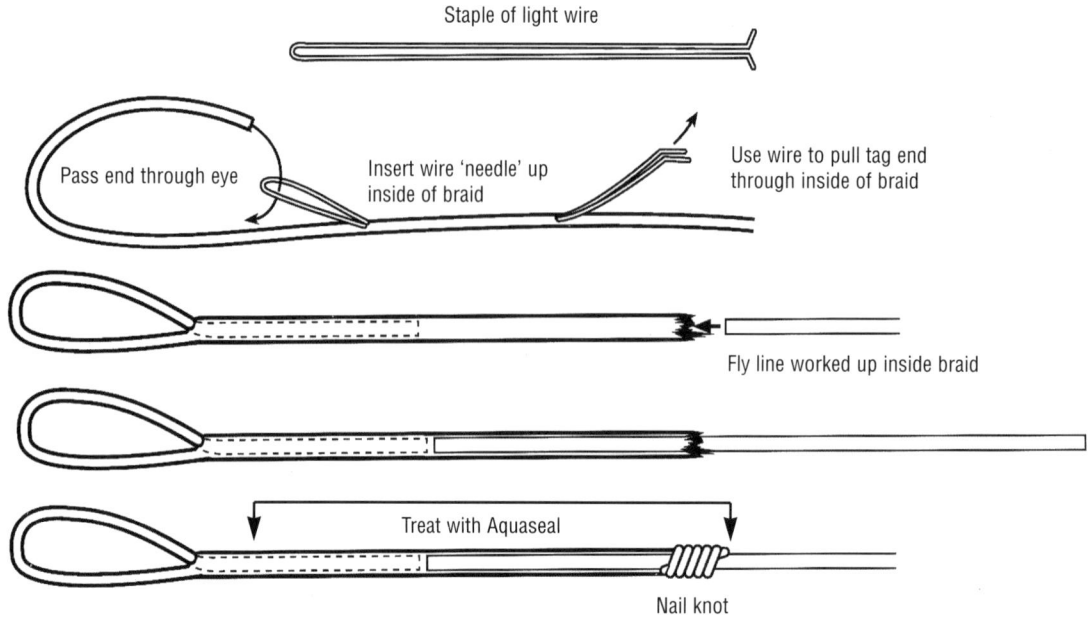

Diagram 7: Braided mono end loop

There are two possibilities here. Many shooting lines are made of the hollow circular braided mono that we have just used to cushion the superbraid loop. In this case we can simply splice a loop in the end. Use the section of doubled-over wire: pass it up the centre of the braided mono and use it as a needle to pull the tag end down the inside for about 50 mm and out through the side wall, forming a loop in the end. About 20 mm further down, pull the tag end back into the centre of the standing line and run it down another 50 mm and out through the side wall again. Trim the tag end off, and snug it back inside. Add a smear of Aquaseal to several sections of the splice, then let it dry.

The second possibility is when you are using a full-length (for example, a weight-forward line) fly line, or a type of shooting line that is like a fine-diameter plastic-coated fly line. We can extend the system of braided mono loops here. Splice a loop in the end of a section of the braided mono material as before, but after forming the loop pull the tag end down inside the standing part by about 50 mm, and snug it back inside. Allow about 60 mm below this point and cut the braid.

Now pass the end of the fly line up inside the butt end of the braided mono until it reaches the tag end. Using a length of 6 or 8-kg monofilament, tie a nail knot over the end of the braided mono to secure it to the fly line. Trim any stray spraggs of mono with nail clippers and coat the whole assembly with Aquaseal, from (and including) the nail knot up to where the loop begins.

No doubt you can see the advantages of the braided mono loop system for joining lines.

If you have a braided mono shooting line, just attach it to the shooting head by easing the back end of the shooting head inside the braid for about 50 mm, nail knot where the

Setting up the line and leader

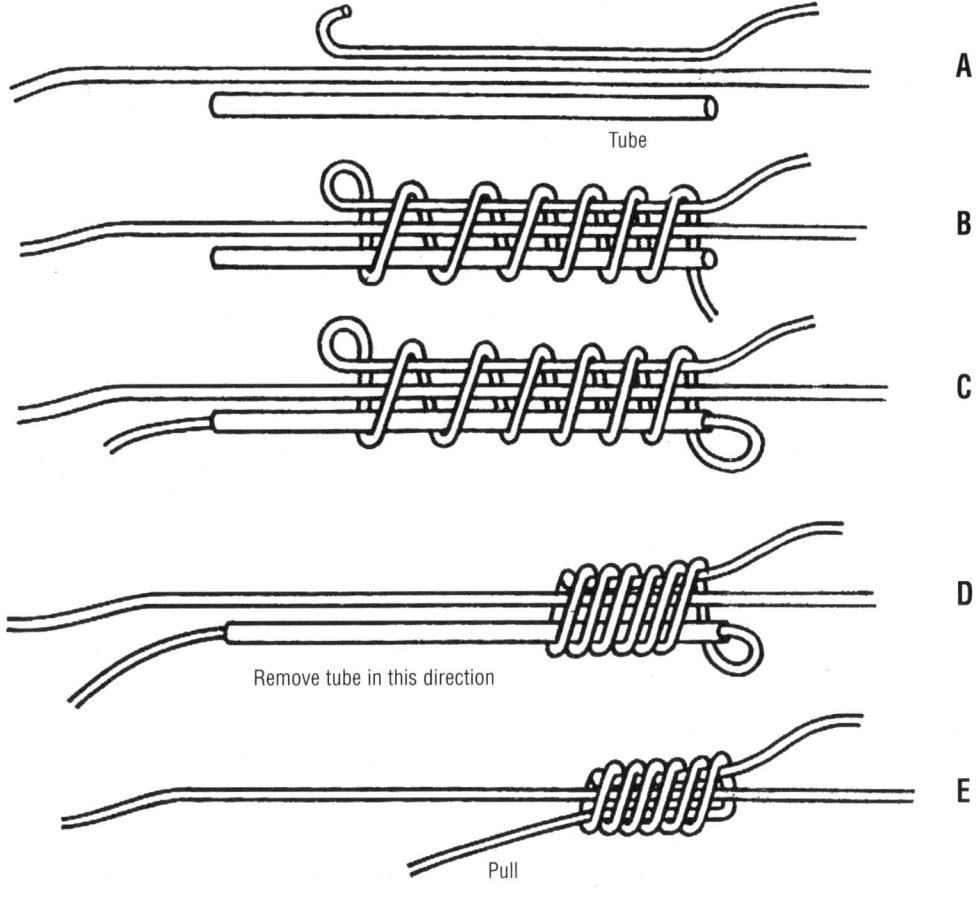

Diagram 8: Nail knot

braid ends on the fly line with monofilament, and coat with Aquaseal.

Now add a further braided mono loop to the front end of the fly line where the leader will be joined in loop-to-loop fashion.

I usually make up a few spare braided mono loops in several sizes of braid to suit different thickness of fly line. I carry these in case I need to replace a loop in a hurry. The pre-formed loop (with the loop end splice already secured with Aquaseal) can be slipped over the end of the fly line, nail knotted on, and a spot of Superglue added (to the nail knot only). Superglue dries much more quickly than Aquaseal, allowing you to get straight back into action. Aquaseal really needs twenty-four hours to cure.

The leader

Now we come into the monofilament section. I am fully aware that there are many knots, designs and techniques for making leaders, but I am also aware just how easy it is for this technical stuff to confuse the reader, so I will try to keep it simple, and you can experiment at your leisure.

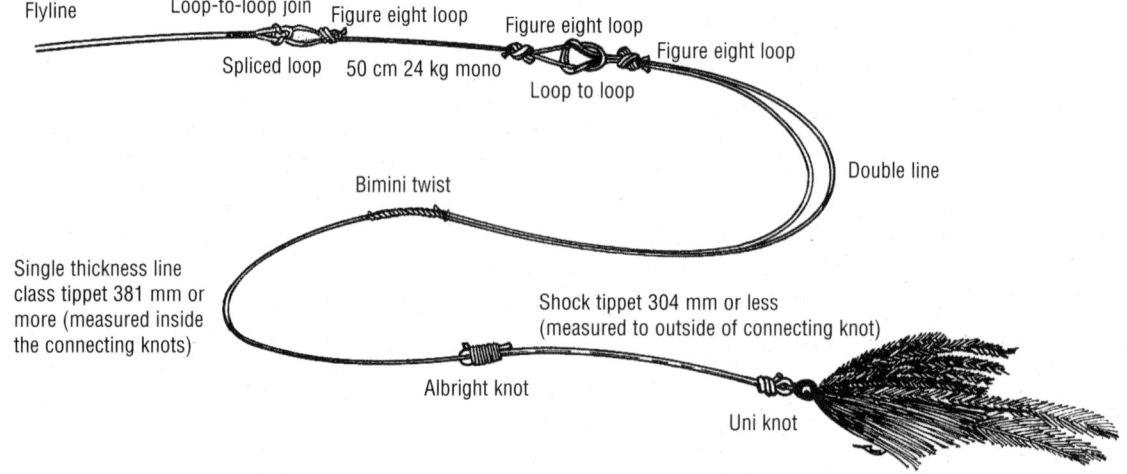

Diagram 9: IGFA legal saltwater fly fishing leader assembly

A very simple leader was described in the first chapter, but there are ways of making much stronger and more adaptable leader systems.

A standard fixture is a short length of heavy-ish monofilament, about half a metre long, as a connection between the fly-line end and the leader proper. It may vary from 10 kg to 24 kg, depending on the magnitude of the tackle, leader, and fish you are targeting. A figure eight loop knot is tied in each end. One end is a loop-to-loop connection to the fly line, the other a loop-to-loop connection to the leader. Again, this is a way of stepping up and down the line diameters so there is not too radical a difference that can cause one to cut into another: for example, a fine mono leader cutting into the end loop of the fly line.

The next leader section is called the 'class' tippet. This is the section that defines the line 'class' or breaking strain that you are using, and incorporates the weakest part of the assembly. Consider this section to be consumable. Wear and tear, snags, and broken-off fish may cause you to replace this section regularly, which is where the loop-to-loop join with the monofilament section above it comes in handy.

Again, try to keep the line thicknesses at the join reasonably similar so that one will not cut the other. Take the leader material and tie a Bimini twist in one end. Double-back the loop that is formed and tie a figure eight knot in it so each side of the leg is formed of two thicknesses. To save time on the water – when being prepared can mean the difference between catching and missing out – I tie up a bunch of these leaders when I am sitting around at home in front of the TV, put them in individual little zip-lock plastic bags, and mark the bag with an ink marker as to the leader strength.

Minimum leader length by IGFA regulation (see Chapter 6) is 15 ins (38.10 cm) measured inside the knots. Depending on what you are fishing for, you may wish for a longer leader than this, although there is no need to go to the excesses of freshwater leaders. If you are pre-making leaders, it pays to leave plenty of line to tie onto the shock tippet (which we will come to in a moment).

I often do not use a shock tippet when having a fun session with a bunch of kahawai

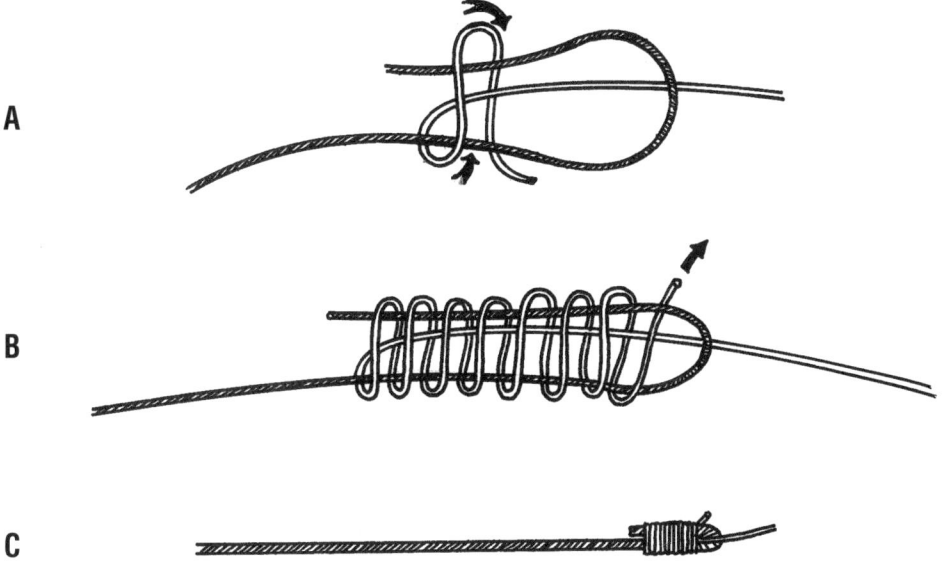

Diagram 10: Albright knot

or trevally, but just re-tie the fly knot regularly. Leaving the thicker shock tippet (to which we are, by degrees, coming) out of the equation will get you more strikes, especially with fish 'krilling' on the surface. To avoid changing leaders all the time, I may start with a leader that is 2 m long or more; this allows for a number of fly changes or knot re-ties before it is too short to be useful.

Finally, we come to the shock tippet. This is a short (12 ins, or 30.48 cm measured outside the knots, if you are fishing to regulation) section of leader material, allowed to protect the class tippet from the teeth and jaws of a fish. It can be made of any material, but heavier mono, fluorocarbon or wire are usual. Depending on thickness and material, different systems can be used to connect the class tippet to the shock tippet. I find that a well-tied albright knot is fine in most situations.

If wire is required (for sharks or barracouta), I use plastic-coated types, and form a loop in the end with a crimp, or cigarette lighter in the case of the Lockweld or Twistweld material. Because the wire has a plastic coating, the mono leader can be tied straight to it with an albright knot without the problem of the mono wearing on the wire.

If I am using very heavy mono shock leader, I crimp a small solid ring to the end, and tie the class tippet to this with a uni knot.

The final connection is to the fly. This can be done simply with a uni knot or improved clinch knot. In cable or heavy mono, a crimp can be used. The action of a fly in the water is improved if it is free to move on a loop, and this can sometimes make a difference. A fixed loop is best made with Lefty's loop knot or a uni knot that has been tightened but not fully pulled up to the fly. This has the advantage of pulling up tight after the fish is hooked, and avoids the hook eye chafing the loop during the fight.

Saltwater Fly Fishing in New Zealand

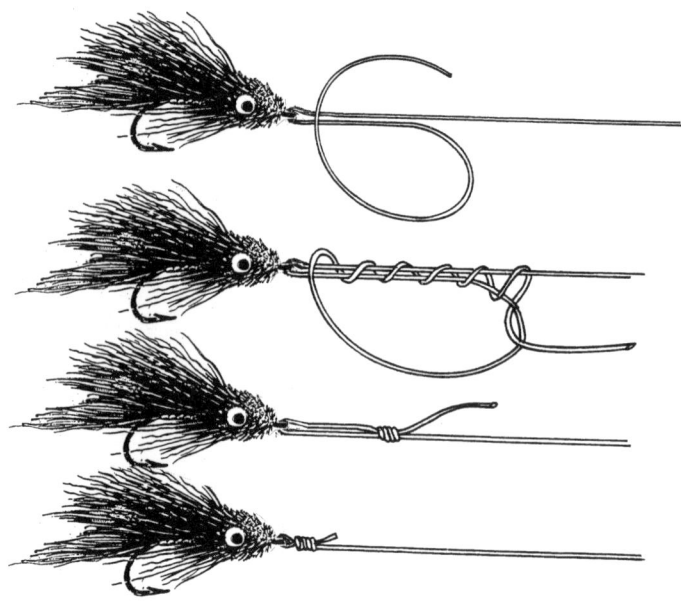

Diagram 11: Uni knot

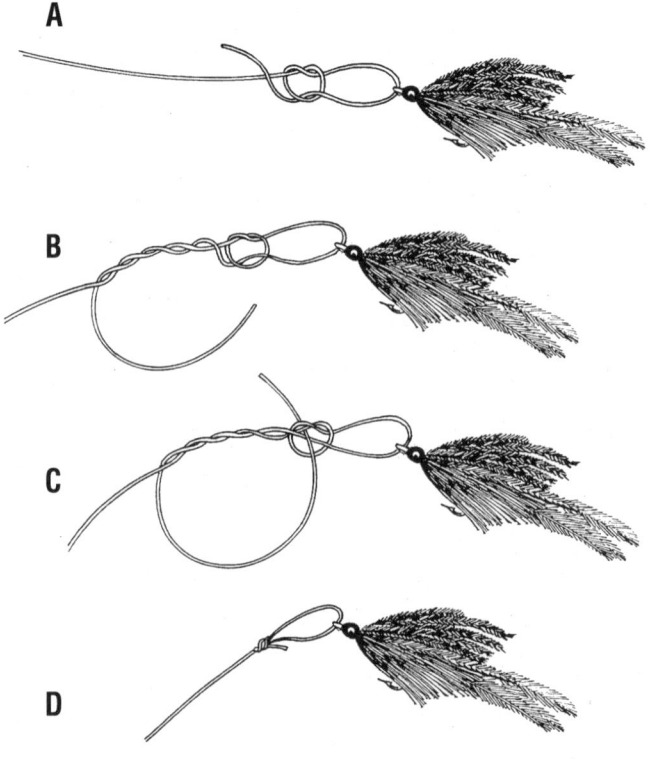

Diagram 12: Lefty's loop

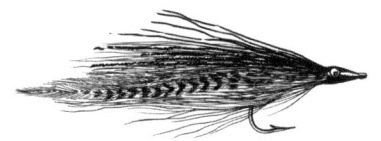

4
Casting

As mentioned earlier, one of the main differences between casting with a fly rod and casting with conventional tackle is that, with standard casting gear, the weight of the lure, sinker or bait pulls the line from the reel; when fly fishing, it is the weight of the line that carries the fly.

Fly rodding had its birth on the fresh waters of England as a system of delivering a near-weightless insect imitation to feeding trout. Put simply, the rod is used as a catapult to throw a line in the manner of a stock whip, and the line carries the fly with it.

When casting a fly, timing and technique are everything. With half an hour's practice, anyone (apart from those whose co-ordination is seriously challenged) should be able to cast 15 m of line. At the other end of the scale, very good casters may be able to put out 35 m in sympathetic conditions. However, add 15 knots of head wind and a fly the size of a small budgie, and the 35-m cast can suddenly become a 20-m cast.

Although you can still catch fish on fly with relatively short casts, and I have seen anglers who can't cast at all catch fish, it is certainly no disadvantage to be able to cast well. There are times when being able to reach right out there can make all the difference, such as when trying to present a fly to a school of spooky trevally or fast-moving skipjack. Casting ability will also help you cope with wind and larger flies.

Making a good cast relies on the correct loading and unloading of the rod. It does not matter how strong you are; timing is the important thing. You will often hear the term 'effortless casting', and a good cast will feel like that – effortless.

The correct loading of a rod is easier to feel if the rod is well over-lined; that is, if it has a line several weights heavier than it was rated for – just for practice purposes (although I am not suggesting that you should buy a line just for this). Working such a rig backwards and forwards will help you get a feel for the rod loading and unloading as you make casting strokes.

Basic casting

American SWF icon Lefty Kreh is credited with distilling the modern approach to casting techniques, and much of what follows is based on his teaching.

Ease of casting and distance of cast are related to the speed at which the line travels. The faster the rod moves, the more it loads and works for you. Also, the further the rod

The line must have all the slack pulled out before the cast begins.

The rod begins to load as the back cast starts.

Back-cast rod movement completed and the back-cast line loop begins to form.

The back cast starts to straighten out behind and the forward cast begins.

moves, the more energy it imparts to the line. Don't be afraid to use your whole arm in the cast. The old training technique of holding a rolled newspaper between your elbow and side while learning to cast has long been discredited.

Achieving good line speed begins with the start of the cast. The line cannot be lifted with the rod until all the slack is pulled out of it. Strip in line until it lies straight between the fly and the rod tip. As you make the pick-up, start with the rod tip pointing at the water to allow for maximum rod movement. Don't try to pick up too much line with the rod or you will not get a clean start to the cast.

As you make the stroke for the back cast, the rod loads. As just mentioned, the faster and the further the rod moves, the faster and easier the line moves.

Stop the arm movement and the rod stops and straightens out, catapulting the line backwards. As the line straightens out behind, make the forward cast. Speed up the arm movement and stop with your wrist stiff until the final movement of cast – a forward stab with the wrist. The shorter this final wrist movement, the tighter the delivery loop will be,

Casting

The forward cast loads the rod.

The rod unloads its energy and the forward-cast line loop starts to form.

The caster makes the final 'wrist stab' and shoots the line.

and the less resistance is offered by any wind to the forward-moving loop of line. The direction in which the rod stops will determine the direction in which the cast goes.

By making back and forward casts – 'false casts' – you can work out more and more line by releasing line on the forward cast (and, with practice, the back cast as well), without actually making the delivery cast. However, the less false casting you do, the better. It wastes time, and if you are trying to cast to fast-moving fish, this can be critical.

Loading the rod

It is important to have the correct amount of line out to load the rod properly for the final line shoot. Too much line and the rod will overload and you lose line speed; too little line out and you will not achieve optimum load on the rod, and casting distance will suffer again.

This correct loading of the rod is easy with shooting heads: you should have the shooting head just out of the rod tip. Many weight-forward lines now incorporate a

Saltwater Fly Fishing in New Zealand

The first haul on the line is made as the line is lifted from the surface.

As the back cast is made the line hand drifts toward the rod hand.

The back cast is completed and the forward cast is about to begin.

The second haul on the line is made to increase line speed as the forward cast begins.

The forward cast loads the rod.

The line is released and shot through the open fingers of the line hand.

colour change where the head of the line ends, making it easy again. You may wish to find this point and mark it with a spirit marker on your line as an aid. Eventually you will be able to tell when the correct amount of line is out of the rod tip, just from the feel.

When making the final cast, think in terms of ballistics. As you would do to get maximum distance out of a bullet or an arrow, make your delivery cast a rising one.

Line hauls

To further increase your line speed, and hence your casting distance, you can incorporate into your cast what is called a haul, or better yet, the double haul. A single haul is achieved like this: as you start to make the back cast with your rod, make a strip of the line held in your other hand. This is a single haul, and helps with line acceleration and rod loading. Now, as the back cast is made, drift your line hand back up towards your rod hand and, as you make the forward cast, haul down on the line again; make the forward cast and shoot the line. When you can make these two hauls – the double haul – in sequence, you will find your casting distance will increase, and the amount of false casting much reduced.

Casting shooting heads

A shooting head, as previously explained, is a short, heavy section of fly line with a much lighter length of 'shooting line' attached to the back. The head section of this assembly is false cast until the connection with the lighter shooting line is just out of the rod tip. This should be accomplished in one or two false casts. A quick double haul is made to increase line speed, then the line is shot on the forward cast. The heavy shooting head tows the light shooting line out, allowing greater casting distance with less false casts. This assembly tends to sink quicker than a conventional fly line, and the reduced back-cast length also allows easier casting in confined spaces.

For the shore-based angler, a shooting basket strapped around the waist is an ideal way to contain the line when wading or rock fishing.

On the water

Casting practice on the grass can be a different bucket of meat to being out there on the water, putting theory into practice. Wind is probably one of the most frustrating aspects. The more powerful rods and heavier lines used at sea are an aid here. Try and position yourself or your boat so that the wind is helping rather than hindering your casting.

When fishing out of a boat, you may have two or more anglers wanting to cast in the same direction – usually astern down a berley trail, or towards a structure. If the anglers are all right-handers, there are several ways to work. In a larger boat, you can work in a circular manner, each angler casting in turn from the right-hand corner of the cockpit (looking astern), then moving to the left to make the retrieve, making room for the next angler.

This is OK if you are using a shooting basket to contain the retrieved line and move it with you, but may not work so well if you are stripping line in, onto the cockpit floor.

A more sensible system, especially when fishing blind from smaller boats, is for the angler on the 'off' side of the boat to cast facing the bow, and to lay out their back cast rather than the forward cast.

Fly lines can be like living entities at times. If there is anything available for the line to catch or tangle on, it will do so. Screw heads, catches, rocks, plants, bags, big toes, sandal straps or shoe laces all seem to leap out and grab the line, just as you make the big shoot.

It is well worthwhile removing potential obstacles to casting before you start. Using a container, such as a fish bin or laundry basket, to strip the line into is a good idea. In boats, sticking masking or packing tape over catches and cleats can help. Another help is to spread a cast net or big sack over the area in which you are working.

More mobile anglers, on the shore or in a boat, can use a large shooting basket. This is a basket strapped to the angler's waist into which the line is stripped during the retrieve. Commercial models are available, or a makeshift model can be made from a belt looped through a plastic basket of some type, such as a small laundry basket. There are plenty to choose from at large plastic supply stores.

If you are working a specific spot, such as a rocky point, a wetted-down sack, towel, or old blanket may make a suitable surface on to which to strip your line, to avoid the rough rock surface catching the line, and also damaging the finish.

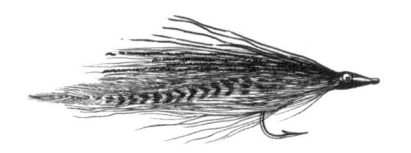

5
Flies and fly tying

Harking back to the freshwater origins of flies, the idea of the near-weightless construction of hook, feather and fur was to imitate the natural food on which the trout was feeding, and fool it into taking – 'matching the hatch', as it is now referred to.

In salt water there is a huge range of fish, and a massive number of prey items. Flies might range from tiny shrimp patterns up to the 30-cm-long monsters needed to mimic the baitfish on which marlin feed.

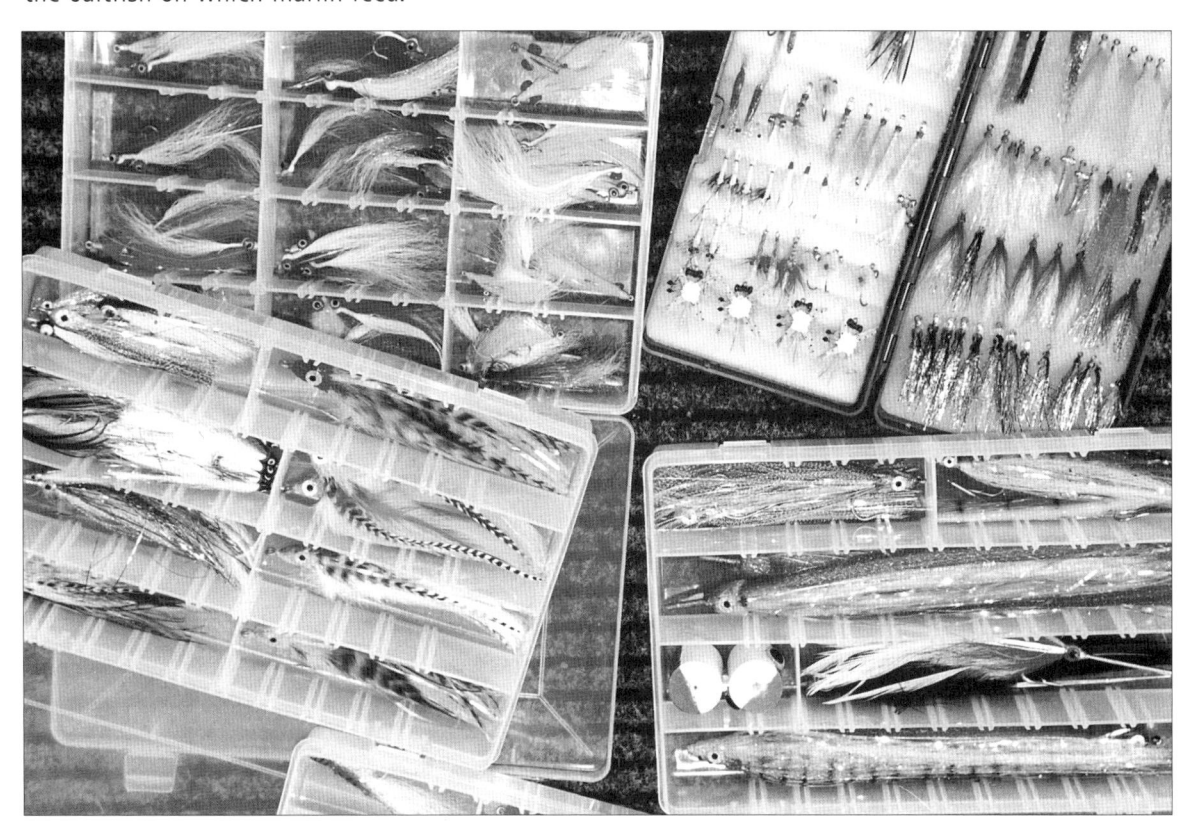

Saltwater flies may imitate anything from a small crustacean to a large baitfish.

Although there are occasions when saltwater fish will grab anything that is thrown in the water, more often the 'match the hatch' practice applies to SWF as well. Get the size, colour and presentation right and success will be greatly improved.

There are two ways to acquire flies: buy them, or tie them yourself (a third way is to pinch them off your mates). With the increasing popularity of SWF, more shops are carrying at least a basic range of patterns and sizes, with some specialist tackle stores having quite a wide range of off-the-shelf patterns to choose from.

Materials

Tying saltwater flies is a lot of the fun – a hobby in itself – and most tackle stores carry fly-tying supplies. In recent times there has been a strong swing to synthetic fly-tying materials, with perhaps only bucktail (deer hair), marabou, and hackle feathers from roosters being the only natural materials regularly used in saltwater flies. Even bucktail is being edged out of the market by synthetic hair materials as their properties become closer to the real thing.

The new-generation materials offer a huge range of colours, flashy finishes and textures, as well as being rot and stain resistant. They come under many names, often different for the same product, and new materials or variations of them hit the market regularly. Names like flashabou, crystal flash, aurora, mylar, fishair, ultra hair, and many others are becoming well known.

Hooks are usually stainless or have strong corrosion-resistant finishes to combat the corrosion caused by salt water. Standard fly-tying thread can be used, although I prefer to use 'invisible' sewing thread (actually very fine monofilament) as it can be used anywhere on the fly without showing up.

To make the fly as robust as possible, I also use dabs of Superglue at key construction points, and finish most of my fly heads with five-minute epoxy glue, either Crystal Clear, or Z-Poxy, which stays clear in the long term, while other types may yellow. You may have to turn the fly around manually to prevent the glue from sagging until it stiffens up. I have adapted a small battery-run hobby engine to turn the flies slowly. It is simpler, of course, to use standard head cement or several coats of nail varnish.

Also available are a wide range of eyes for flies, including stick-on types, movable dolls' eyes, dumb-bell types in lead, tungsten, copper and brass, bead chain eyes (the same stuff as used on bathroom plugs), and cast resin. Most of these need securing with a coat of epoxy over the top. Other add-ons are different types of metal and glass beads that are slipped over the hook point and secured up behind the eye of the hook. These are used to add colour, flash and sometimes weight to a fly.

Six of the best

The range of potential patterns can be multiplied by a wide range of sizes, and again by colour combinations. Whole books have been written on fly patterns, so with limited space I will outline half a dozen styles of fly which I have found to be the most useful. I say 'styles', as a basic construction technique is frequently varied in terms of material and colour and renamed. By learning a handful of general tying techniques, then changing the size, colour, materials and bulk of these general patterns, a wide range of flies may be created which will cover all but the most specialised of applications.

Clouser's minnow

This fly was designed by American Bob Clouser, with input from Lefty Kreh. Kreh passed on the pattern to Australian SWF pioneer Rod Harrison, and in about 1987 Rod gave me a couple of prototypes. The two all-white flies caught me eleven trevally and three snapper in sessions at Little Barrier and the Mokohinaus before I lost them, and have been a mainstay pattern for me ever since.

Small versions bounced along the bottom have a crustacean-like appearance. Larger models are a fair baitfish imitation.

Clouser's minnow

This fly is tied reversed: the weighted eyes are tied on top of the hook so that the fly rides point up when retrieved. This results in much less snagging when fished along the bottom.

This is a very flexible pattern, and if I could use only one type of fly for SWF, Clouser's minnow would be the one.

Hook: I like a bit of bend back in the hook for this pattern, and use the Gamakatsu SC-15 or Black Magic 2546 after adding a slight bend to the shank. For very large models I use a Gamakatsu SL12S. Sizes may vary from 8 to 8/0.

Eyes: Weighted dumb-bell type: lead, tungsten, or bead-chain. These are tied on top of the hook so that the fly rides point up. To help support the eyes, build up two bulges of tying thread for the eyes to nestle between, then cross-lash them down well. Add a drop of Superglue. The fly eyes should be about 3–4 mm behind the eye of the hook.

Wing: With the hook still point down in the vice, tie in a fairly sparse bunch of white bucktail or fishair on top of the hook, in front of the dumb-bell eyes. Take the thread back and lash the hair down just behind the eyes as well. Turn the fly over in the vice (eyes down, point up). Tie in a further wing of hair or bucktail in front of the dumb-bell eyes so that it flares back up towards the hook point. You can add a topping of contrasting-coloured hair, and a few strands of flash material. Good colours are all-white, white and chartreuse, white and red, or white and pink.

Lefty's deceiver

It's that man Kreh again. Lefty's deceiver, often just called the deceiver, is one of the most widely used fly patterns in SWF along with Clouser's minnow. A general baitfish pattern, it can be tied in many colour combinations and different sizes, and can be slim or bulky, weighted or unweighted, to imitate many different baitfish. I once caught a kahawai, a 'rat' kingfish and a snapper in four casts on the same deceiver, illustrating the pattern's wide appeal.

Lefty's deceiver

The general proportions are that the finished fly should be two-and-a-half to three times the length of the hook, and that the collar should extend back past the hook.

Hook: Standard streamer-style hook, such as the Black Magic 2546, Gamakatsu SS15, or Mustad 34007.

Tail: four to twelve white saddle hackles (depending on fly size) paired and tied in at the bend of the hook. A single dyed grizzle hackle (colour to match topping – the natural [grey] grizzle hackle is usually used on the all-white version) is tied in outside each side of these tail hackles. Add about half a dozen strands of crystal flash or flashabou and a dab of Superglue to the binding.

Collar: White bucktail is best, or synthetic hair can be used. Tie in three bunches to the front of the hook, one to each side, then one on top. Add a short throat of red to imitate gills.

Topping: Use dyed bucktail or synthetic hair to match the coloured hackles on the tail. Peacock herl is used on the white and olive version. A few strands of flash material can also be added.

Surf candy

Developed by American tier Bob Popovics, this is a great baitfish imitation that can be altered in colour and size to copy many different types of species. One of this pattern's assets is that it is very robust and will last well over quite a number of fish. I have had great success on kahawai with green and white, and found that blue and white is a real killer on skipjack tuna and albacore when they are meatballing anchovies. Tiny versions match larval fish.

Hook: Standard streamer-style hook, such as the Black Magic 2546, Gamakatsu SS15, or Mustad 34007.

Wing: This is tied from the head: white bucktail or synthetic hair under the hook, with contrasting hair and/or flashabou on top. Add half a dozen or so strands of flash material, such as crystal flash, to each side.

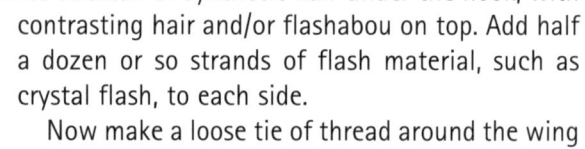

Now make a loose tie of thread around the wing behind the hook to bundle the material in preparation for the addition of the epoxy to the head. Some fly tiers like to do the epoxy in two layers, and this does give a prettier result, but I am too impatient, and consider flies to be cannon fodder anyway. I attach stick-on eyes with a dab of Superglue on the back to hold them in place while I add a single coat of five-minute epoxy. Coat the

Surf candy

epoxy back to the level where the hook emerges from the body. Rotate the fly while it is drying, and just when the glue starts to stiffen, pull the tail of the fly to streamline the form down.

A final touch, after the glue hardens, is to paint red gill slashes with a spirit marker or hobby paint.

Shark fly

One of the biggest problems with fly fishing for sharks is the IGFA regulation that limits shock tippets to 30.48 cm (12 ins). This is assuming that you wish to fish to regulation, and we shall come to this in the next chapter. With only a 30-cm shock tippet (and we are talking wire here), the great danger is that your monofilament class tippet can easily be worn through by contact with a shark's sandpaper skin and fins. The idea, then, is to get as much protection for the mono as possible, within the IGFA regulations.

The other prime criterion for shark flies is the appearance of bulk. If you want to catch what, to a fly fisher, is a decent shark (although it may still be considered a 'rat' by a gamefisherman), you need a fly that represents a worthwhile feed. More of this in Chapter 15 on fly rodding sharks.

My initial answer to minimising the wear problem was to tie my flies on the back end of a single long-shanked hook, which added about another 5 cm of steel to the 30 cm of shock tippet. But as my mate, professional fly tier Pat Swift, pointed out, IGFA regulations allow two hooks, with the eyes a maximum of 6 ins (15 cm) apart. By using a long-shanked hook as the back hook, in practice you can add another 25 cm to the rig, making a total of 55 cm.

Hook: I use two Mustad 8318 7/0 hooks for big flies and a single hook for medium sizes. This is the same hook that is popular for blue cod bait fishing

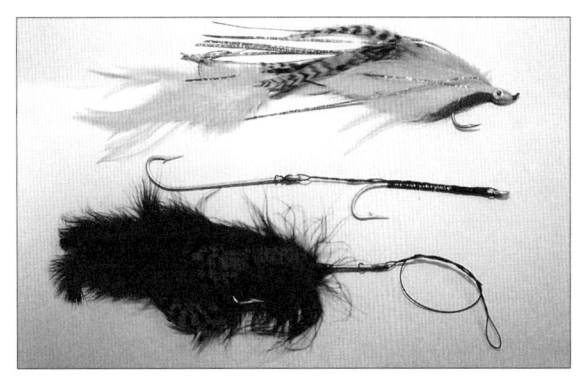

(Top) Double-hooked shark fly (Pat Swift); (middle) Shark fly hook rig; (bottom) Single-hook shark fly.

in the South Island. Before tying the fly, I file down the point, which shortens it and lowers the barb, and put four cutting edges on the hook. This makes the fly much easier to set in tough shark skin with a fly rod and greatly increases the hook-up rate. You will still lose numbers of sharks through leader damage, but with the plating filed off, the hook will rust out more quickly. To protect the hook from corrosion until it is used, paint the exposed steel with a spirit marker.

To connect the two hooks I use 80-lb Halco Lockweld Wire, or crimped cable. Lockweld is a plastic-coated cable that is twisted together and welded in place by melting the plastic coating with a cigarette lighter.

Make sure the hook eyes are well closed before connecting them with wire. I like to make a figure eight turn of the wire around the hook shanks before crimping or welding, to stiffen the fly. Now take some reasonably heavy thread and bind the wire to the shank of the top hook from the eye to opposite the point. Add Superglue to this binding. With this assembly complete you are ready to start tying the fly.

Wings: The arrangement doesn't have to be too sophisticated, and needs be no more than bunches of chook feathers tied to each hook. When fished to sharks that have been attracted to a berley trail, it probably just represents a hunk of something that might be edible – so they bite it.

Some strips of flash material and some contrasting feathers will add to the look of the fly. Start the top fly about halfway down the shank, but use the whole of the lower hook, and be sure to put some solid lashing over the wire twists under the eye. Finish all the exposed bindings with five-minute epoxy. When finished, twist the wire so that the hooks are facing at 180° to each other. Be sure to twist the wire up rather than untwist it.

These are good flies on which to use up junky old feathers. Processed sheep wool or other hair materials can also be substituted or added. Good colours are combinations of yellow, red, white and fawn.

Berley fly

This is 'match the hatch' with a difference. Many species of fish can be attracted by minced berley and small cubes of fish. To catch these fish it is often necessary to use a fly that is an imitation of the chunks of berley and fish the fly by dead-drifting it in the berley trail. I have tried various materials, including marabou and wool, but find egg yarn (glow bug material) to be best in a colour to match the berley. Salmon egg, orange, red and brown are useful, and can be mixed together. When bound down, this material flares away from the hook, and when the length of the hook shank has been packed, may be trimmed to the desired size and shape with a pair of sharp scissors.

Hook: many types can be used, but I like the Black Magic 1920 2X as it has a short but thick shank. This adds strength, and also weight to the fly, giving a more natural drift. Adding weighted eyes can be useful for this fly, as they tend to take quite a while to become totally saturated enough to sink naturally.

A berley or cube fly

Super shrimp

This is a pattern of my own, first published back in 1985 in my first book, *Saltwater Sportfishing*. Draper's Tackle House picked it up from there and supplied it commercially to tackle stores. Since then, I have made a few refinements as new materials have become available.

Hook: long-shank streamer hook such as Black Magic 2546, Gamakatsu SS15, Mustad 34007, or Partridge J.S. Sea Streamer; sizes 2 – 8.

Thread: Invisible sewing thread or other transparent thread.

Head: This fly is tied with the head at the rear of the hook. First tie in ten to twelve pieces of stiff-ish nylon hair, such as nylotail or bristles, extending at least the length of

Flies and fly tying

the hook past the bend. Add to each side a nylon blob eye. These are made by burning the end of a piece of 24-kg mono into a black blob. A brief brush with the flame behind the blob will give a bend which will stand the eye off the hook shank. Now tie in a piece of clear swannundaze and a soft saddle hackle. Tie off the thread and cut, leaving a 300-mm piece dangling for later use. Add a drop of Superglue to the binding.

Super shrimp

Body: Wind the saddle hackle palmer-wise up the body to the hook eye and tie off with a new piece of thread. Follow with the swannundaze, winding through and between the hackle fibres, and tie off just behind the hook eye.

Carapace: I used to make this from a section of plastic drinking straw, but now there are sheets of translucent, slightly holographic plastic available from fly-tying material suppliers. Cut a body shape with a triangular tail narrowing to a 'wrist', slowly widening then tapering away to a point which will protrude back between the eyes. Tie down the 'wrist' on top of the hook, just behind the hook eye, and cut off the thread. Now take the thread left dangling at the other end of the fly and bind down the other end of the body just behind the eyes. Tie off, then spiral the thread down the body and finish off at the hook eye again.

Finishing: A thin coat of Z-Poxy along the carapace will make the fly more robust. Add some stripes to the feelers with a black felt-tip pen; you can darken up the eye blobs too if necessary. Trim the length of the hackle from short at the hook-eye end, and leave longest around the hook-point end.

The colour of this fly is determined by the hackle. Use natural grizzle for a white/clear shrimp; pink, red (for krill imitations), chartreuse, brown or yellow are other good colours.

Popper heads

In limiting this chapter to six of the most useful patterns, I have made no mention of floating 'popper' flies. This is because I have generally been much more successful with subsurface flies. Sometimes kingfish will show a preference for popping over subsurface flies, but mostly I doubt the value of popper flies in the New Zealand situation. Sure, surface strikes are exciting, but because of the light, buoyant nature of these flies, a bow-wave caused by attacking fish often knocks the fly out of the way and the strike is missed. If used with a sinking line, the belly that develops between fly and rod often means missed strikes. Finally, the popping head can tend to guard the hook point, causing more missed strikes.

Still, it is nice to have every avenue covered. Rod Harrison put me onto a system that provides easy

Popping heads can be slipped on the leader above the fly to convert them to surface poppers.

45

back-up. By making up some separate popping heads, and drilling a hole through the middle, any fly can be converted into a popper just by threading the head onto the leader above the fly.

These heads are easily made from cork, EVA, or round sticks of ethafoam, a lightweight packing material. It can be cut to shape with a razor blade, and the hole drilled with a hot wire. Colour can be added with an ink marker if required.

Throw a few of these into the fly box and you cover the possibility of needing popper flies.

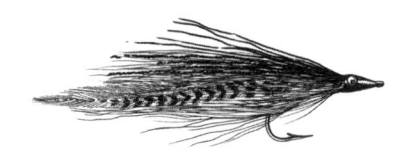

6
Fishing to regulation

Every game must have rules, and saltwater fly fishing is no exception. Unified SWF record keeping and regulation began back in 1960 with an organisation called the Saltwater Fly Rodders of America, who handed the task of record keeping and regulation on to the International Game Fish Association in 1978.

Since then there have been only minor changes to these internationally accepted regulations, with the addition of several new tippet classes and separate records for women to the record books. The IGFA regulations for fly fishing are easy to comply with in regard to fishing for species such as kahawai, trevally and so on, but were penned in an era when taking big gamefish on a fly was not thought of, and make the taking of billfish, sharks and large tuna on fly a real challenge, and a great achievement. Although there has been some pressure to change the regulations to make the capture of big fish easier, many SWF anglers seem to be opposed to this as it would devalue the efforts of previous anglers, and also rob captures of big fish of some of their merit.

Do you have to fish to regulation? Certainly not, if you really don't want to. No one is going to dictate how you fish, but most SWF anglers choose to for a number of good reasons:

• Fishing to regulation establishes a level playing field for all anglers against which they can measure their achievements.
• Most club contests and tournaments are governed by IGFA regulations, and if you are used to fishing this way, you will have no problems at tournament time.
• National and world-record claim fish must be caught to regulation to be considered for records.
• The IGFA regulations really define the parameters of the sport: what is SWF, and what is just fishing with funny tackle.

Following are the IGFA rules for fly fishing, published with the permission of that organisation.

Rules for fly fishing
Equipment regulations

A. LINE
Any type of fly line and backing may be used. The breaking strength of the fly line and backing are not restricted.

B. LEADER

Leaders must conform to generally accepted fly-fishing customs. A leader includes a class tippet and, optionally, a shock tippet. A butt or taper section between the fly line and the class tippet shall also be considered part of the leader and there are no limits on its length, material, or strength.

A class tippet must be made of non-metallic material and either attached directly to the fly or to the shock tippet if one is used. The class tippet must be at least 15 ins (38.10 cm) long (measured inside connecting knots). With respect to knot-less, tapered leaders, the terminal 15 ins (38.10 cm) will also determine tippet class. There is no maximum length limitation.

A shock tippet is not to exceed 12 ins (30.48 cm) in length, and may be added to the class tippet and tied to the lure. It can be made of any type of material, and there is no limit on its breaking strength. The shock tippet is measured from the eye of the hook to the single strand of class tippet, and includes any knots used to connect the shock tippet to the class tippet.

In the case of a tandem-hook fly, the shock tippet shall be measured from the eye of the leading hook.

C. ROD

Regardless of material used or number of sections, rods must conform to generally accepted fly-fishing customs and practices. A rod shall not measure less than 6 ft (1.82 m) in overall length. Any rod that gives the angler an unsporting advantage will be disqualified. Extension butts are limited to 6 ins (15.24 cm).

D. REEL

The reel must be designed expressly for fly fishing. There are no restrictions on gear ratio or type of drag employed, except where the angler would gain an unfair advantage. Electric or electronically operated reels are prohibited.

E. HOOKS

A conventional fly may be dressed on a single or double hook or two single hooks in tandem. The second hook in any tandem fly must not extend beyond the wing material. The eyes of the hooks shall be no farther than 6 ins (15.24 cm) apart. Treble hooks are prohibited.

F. LURES

The lure must be a recognised type of artificial fly, which includes streamer, bucktail, tube fly, wet fly, dry fly, nymph, popper and bug. The use of any other type of lure or natural or preserved bait, either singularly or attached to the fly, is expressly prohibited. The fact that a lure can be cast with a fly rod is not evidence in itself that it fits the definition of a fly. The use of any lure designed to entangle or foul-hook a fish is prohibited. No scent, either natural or artificial, is allowed on flies. The use of scented material in a fly is prohibited.

G. GAFFS & NETS

Gaffs and nets used to boat or land a fish must not exceed 8 ft (2.44 m) in overall length. (When fishing from a bridge, pier or other high stationary structure, this length limitation does not apply.) The use of a flying gaff is not permitted.

Only a single hook is permitted on any gaff. Harpoon or lance attachments are prohibited. A rope or any extension cannot be attached to the gaff.

Careful measurement of leader length ensured no worries for Carl Angus after the capture of this mako, for several years the world record on 4-kg tippet.

This 28-kg kingfish, a tremendous capture off the rocks on fly, could not be claimed for the world record because the angler had used a shock tippet 4 cm over the permitted length. Photo: Mark Draper

Angling regulations

1. The angler must cast, hook, fight, and bring the fish to gaff or net unaided by any other person. No other person may touch any part of the tackle during the playing of the fish or give aid other than taking the leader for gaffing or netting purposes.
2. Casting and retrieving must be carried out in accordance with normal customs and generally accepted practices. The major criterion in casting is that the weight of the line must carry the fly, rather than the weight of the fly carry the line. Trolling a fly behind a moving water craft is not permitted. The craft must be completely out of gear, both at the time the fly is presented to the fish and during the retrieve. The maximum amount of line that can be stripped off the reel is 120 ft (36.57 m) from the fly.
3. Once a fish is hooked, the tackle may not be altered in any way, with the exception of adding an extension butt.
4. Fish must be hooked on the fly in use. If a small fish takes the fly and a large fish swallows the smaller fish, the catch will be disallowed.
5. One of more people may assist in gaffing or netting the fish.
6. The angling and equipment regulations shall apply until the fish is weighed.

The following acts will disqualify a catch:

1. Failure to comply with equipment or angling regulations.
2. The act of persons other than the angler in touching any part of the rod, reel, or line, either bodily or with any device during the playing of the fish, or in giving aid other than that allowed in the rules and regulations. If an obstacle to the passage of the line through the rod guides has to be removed from the line, then the obstacle shall be held and cut free. Under no circumstances should the line be held or touched by anyone other than the angler during this process.
3. Resting the rod on any part of the boat, or on any other object while playing the fish.
4. Handlining or using a handline or rope attached in any manner to the angler's line or leader for the purpose of holding or lifting the fish.
5. Intentionally foul-hooking or snagging a fish.
6. Shooting, harpooning, or lancing any fish (including sharks and halibut) at any stage of the catch.
7. Chumming with the flesh, blood, skin or any part of mammals.
8. Using a boat or device to beach or drive a fish into shallow water in order to deprive the fish of its normal ability to swim.
9. Attaching the angler's line or leader to part of a boat or other object for the purpose of holding or lifting the fish.
10. If a fish escapes before gaffing or netting and is recaptured by any method other than as outlined in the angling rules.
11. When a rod breaks (while the fish is being played) in a manner that reduces its length below minimum dimensions or severely impairs its angling characteristics.
12. When a fish is hooked or entangled on more than one line.
13. Mutilation to the fish, prior to landing or boating the catch, caused by sharks, other fish, mammals, or propellers that remove or penetrate the flesh. (Injuries caused by leader or line, scratched, old healed scars or regeneration deformities are not considered to be

disqualifying injuries.) Any mutilation of the fish must be shown in a photograph and fully explained in a separate report accompanying the record application.

The main things to watch here are: the lengths of leader parts; no baiting or scenting of flies; gaff and net length; no flying gaffs (only an issue with gamefish); and trolling is not permitted. Note especially this last one – if you are using a boat, you must make a delivery cast to the fish with the engine out of gear, and it must stay out of gear while the retrieve is made. After the fish is hooked, the boat may be used to chase it if you wish. *Trolling with SWF tackle is not considered to be saltwater fly fishing,* although it can be a lot of fun and a good way of getting a feel of playing fish with fly gear.

In the final analysis, it is not hard to conform, in most cases, to 'the regs' as available tackle fits inside the guidelines. Practically every SWF angler that I have met in this country fishes to IGFA regulation, and would not consider doing otherwise.

7
Small game

In all the challenges and excitement of catching saltwater sportfish on fly, we should never overlook the sheer fun aspects of poking around with fly gear for whatever turns up. I have said it before: to a real fisherman, the most important fish is the one on the end of your line at the time.

As well as the larger and more powerful species that we will deal with later in this book, there are many smaller fish that are fun to catch on light tackle, especially when you scale down to lighter fly rigs like a 5-weight rod with a 2-kg leader.

Common species include the mackerel clan – jack mackerel and koheru; yellow-eye mullet (also called herrings or sprats); piper; blue maomao, pink maomao and their grey lookalike, the sweep. Add to this the wrasses – especially spotties and banded wrasse; jock stewarts; granddaddy hapuku (scorpionfish); juveniles of species like snapper, kahawai, trevally etc; and a whole raft of unusual species that have grabbed my fly at times – butterfly perch, goatfish, spotted stargazer and others – and you can see that there is a big range of potential targets.

The broad brush

Many of these fish will fall to a broad-brush approach – one type of approach can take many different species.

Berley can be a key component for this type of fishing: it will attract fish and hold them in the area you are fishing, and will get them in the feeding mood. The approach is similar whether you

Ross Johnson took this granddaddy hapuku (scorpionfish) on a sinking line in the Bay of Islands.

are fishing from a boat, wharf or rock, although the species may differ.

In the north, typical species would include jack mackerel, koheru, sweep, blue and pink maomao, juvenile kahawai and trevally; and, inshore, piper and yellow-eye mullet.

To the south, warm-water species like maomao and koheru disappear, and members of the wrasse family, particularly the aggressive spotties but also scarlet, girdled, and banded wrasse, fill the niche.

Fly fishing around structures like wharves is a great way to target small game on fly.

Berley can be anything you have to hand, and may also be bought commercially. A good base is old bread, cooked rice or potato, or other starchy material. This will work on its own, but is improved by adding minced or chopped-up fish from, preferably, oily pelagic species. Minced fish will work well on its own as well. Avoid products from deep-sea species such as orange roughy, hoki and the like, as it actually seems to repel other fish.

Berley can be prepared beforehand and frozen (two-litre plastic milk bottles are useful for this). When hung in the water in a mesh bag or in the plastic bottle with a few holes cut in it, it will disperse as it thaws, allowing you to concentrate on fishing, and avoiding the noise of working a berley pot and chopper.

A fresh mulch can be prepared on the spot by mushing up the bread, etc. in a bucket with a little water and fish remains, and then dispersed by regularly spooning or cupping a portion into the water. This is more often done off the rocks, where a backwash can be used to mix and hold a certain amount of berley, providing a more regular trail to open water.

Straight bread, potato, cooked rice or other such material (in the Pacific Islands village fishermen berley by chewing coconut meat and spitting the results into the water) tends to attract more yellow-eye mullet and piper, especially when used in harbours, estuaries, and the tidal sections of rivers. Here, a small 'bread fly' made with cotton wool on a size 12 – 16 hook is effective, fished on a 2-kg leader. These fish will also take freshwater nymph patterns, such as a hare and copper or pheasant tail nymph, in small sizes. These flies are mostly tied on bronzed hooks, however, and after saltwater exposure are pretty much write-offs.

Blue maomao, such as this huge White Island specimen, are a challenge on light fly tackle.

Berleying from boats, especially from dinghies in shallow water, or around offshore islands and reefs will almost inevitably bring in small fish to feed just behind the boat. Small berley flies dead-drifted or sometimes just held in the current can be effective here, as can very small shrimp patterns, small Clouser's minnows, freshwater nymph patterns, and tiny surf candy flies.

My favourite fish here are jack mackerel, their similar-looking but harder-pulling cousins the koheru, and the attractive and tough blue maomao. On scaled-down tackle (4 and 5-weight rods and 1 to 2-kg leaders), they are good sport. The jacks and koheru are useful baitfish, and the maomao a tasty eating fish. Small kahawai and trevally are also common in the berley, and you will sometimes get more than you bargained for if an adult kahawai, big trevally or small kingfish shows up. This is the time to switch to heavier tackle, or accept the challenge on the light gear.

Prospecting

Of course, berley trail fishing is only one aspect of small-game fly fishing. Blind fishing with small flies on sinking lines can turn up all manner of species. I like to use a small Clouser's minnow for this as it is such an adaptable fly. Given a fairly fast retrieve, it is a fair baitfish imitation. Fished along the bottom, the weighted eyes give the fly a hopping action, reminiscent of crab or shrimp, while the hook-up attitude of the fly considerably reduces snagging. Just by varying sink times and retrieve styles I can prospect several different scenarios with the same gear.

Juveniles of popular sportfish, such as this just-legal snapper that Ivan Leslie caught from the Kingfish Lodge wharf, are a common catch for shallow-water fly rodders.

Small game

A few years ago, I headed down to Fiordland to chase bluefin tuna on conventional tackle and, out of interest, packed a fly rod with which to dabble around the sounds and see what sort of fish might be partial to feathers in the deep south.

We were fortunate in that the Johnson and De Rijk packing company offered our hosts, Fiordland crayfishermen Mark Harris and Ron Grant, the use of the accommodation at their crayfish depot on a tiny island in Doubtful Sound. Built on piles between high- and low-water marks, The Blanket Bay Hotel looks like something out of a cross between *Mad Max* and *Waterworld*. But it is warm, dry and sandfly proof, and allowed us to be a lot more comfortable than we would have been crammed together on the boat.

A selection of useful flies for small game. Top: berley flies; second row (L – R): bread fly, freshwater nymph; third row: small surf candies; bottom (L – R): shrimp, small Clouser's minnow.

After we settled in on the first evening, I strung together my fly rod and tied on a white Clouser's minnow. Stepping outside the front door, I found a gap in the beech trees for my back cast and flicked out the fly.

As it sank from sight in the tannin-stained water, it was nailed hard. After its initial dash the fish was easily turned – a large male spotty. As I lifted the fish out of the water to unhook it, it seemed like the whole bottom came with it. A mixed school of maybe 100 fish followed it up, the bolder ones trying to get the fly away from it. The next cast hardly made it below the surface.

What a place – towering mountains cloaked by dense rainforest, a magnificent waterfall crashing into the sea across the gently rippling sound, a soft sunset adding rose and brass blushes to sea and sky, and strike-every-cast fishing at the front doorstep. Then your mate hands you a glass of medicinal port. Perfect!

I left my rod rigged, and every time I had a minute or two to spare during the trip I would make a cast. It was a rare thing to make a retrieve without getting a strike. Initially, the various wrasses, and in particular the spotties, were so voracious that I could not get a fly past them. If I ripped the fly along the surface too fast for them to catch, they slashed at it, and its progress was punctuated by swirls and splashes, like a school of rat kings after a popper.

It was a fascinating fishing. Sure, the fish were small, and even when magnified by the fly rod their struggles seldom took line from my hand. But the hits were hard, and it was always interesting to see what I had caught.

The wrasses seem to occupy a much broader niche in the south, and are much more aggressive. They would attack even quite large flies at the start. The spotties were the boldest – southern piranhas – but when I could get the fly past their cordon by casting well out and letting it sink deep, other species came to light. Banded wrasse and big scarlet wrasse seemed to sit a bit deeper down than the spots, but were just as keen on flies.

The weird and wonderful: the author took this spotted stargazer on a small fly retrieved slowly along the bottom.

Another fish that hung back a bit from the spotty school was a group of butterfly perch. They weren't really keen on the fly, but I would sometimes get a pass out of them on the first cast of a session, before the spotties found out that the game had started and they hadn't got to their seats yet. One evening, as the light was falling, one butterfly made a mistake and was hooked. It was interesting to see the usually bright pinks and purples of this fish in much darker shades, an adaptation to the tea-coloured water in the sounds.

There was a trophy fish in my miniature fishing world. Hanging deep and occasionally coming to the top of the bunch was a gorgeous olive and yellow trumpeter. Beside my gang of wrasses he looked huge, although I doubt if he would have weighed 1 kg. He was interested in the fly, but time after time the spotty hordes would beat him to it.

I persevered on and off, and on about the third day it happened. The spotty defence screen went to sleep for a minute, and like Christian Cullen spotting the gap, the trump was through and about to find out for itself what this fly thing was all about. Considering its size, it fought well, and I had to work to keep it out of the wharf pilings.

After a quick photo, it was returned to the water, like all the other fish. Over a week or so, with just the odd little session mornings and evenings, I probably caught every fish in the bunch several times, and they started to learn. Bit by bit, the interest died down, and my flies could sink through the school unmolested.

Now that I was fishing right along the bottom, I was hoping to catch a blue cod, but the seabed off our little island seemed to be totally lined with jock stewarts, all with their mouths open. Northerners know these fish as sea perch, or scarpies. I fished several other spots around our tiny island where the forest canopy permitted a cast, and it was a jock every cast.

Small game in the south: this little Fiordland trumpeter slipped through the spotties' defensive screen.

Any fish, even the small ones, can be fun on fly.

Above: Sharks that are not in the feeding mood can be teased with natural bait to make them more aggressive.
Below: Surface feeders, like these 'krilling' trevally, provoke that gut feeling of 'I can't miss!', but they can be fussy about what fly they will take.

Above: Mahimahi are an occasional warm-water visitor to northern waters. They eat as good as they fight.
Below left: Blue cod, such as this big Fiordland fish, are suckers for a deeply fished fly.
Below right: Kahawai, like this Hauraki Gulf specimen caught by Richard Dobbinson, are the backbone of New Zealand SWF.

Right: Carl Angus with a home-tied shark fly on a long-shanked hook with a Lockweld wire shock leader. He called it 'Picasso' ... look closely at its eyes ...

Below: An excited mako charges through the berley trail, and never even noticed when it was free-tagged. In this mood you can bet they will jump on any fly presented.

Above: Angler Richard Dobbinson brings his first fly-rod marlin to the boat, while Predator deckie Mike Harris prepares to slip a light gaff over the fish's bill to guide it to the boat for release.

Left: Kingfish are one of the toughest fly-rod opponents, with even the 'rats' giving a great performance.

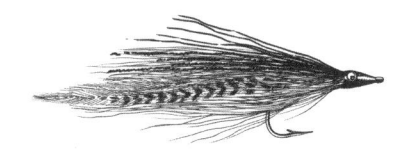

8
Catching kahawai

Taken overall, kahawai are one of the great fly-rod fish. Although they get a hammering from purse-seiners, they can still be found from one end of the country to the other. From the tidal reaches of rivers, out into the blue water, in foaming surface schools, and individual bottom feeders, they will exploit any available niche.

Add to this availability a willingness to take all manner of flies, run hard, jump repeatedly, but fight cleanly, and you have a fish that is the backbone of New Zealand saltwater fly fishing. On top of that, they are good-looking, and a fair table fish as well. Consequently, these enthusiastic fish are the species upon which many anglers start their SWF careers.

From the shore

Kahawai are a very achievable fish for the shore-bound SWF angler. They can be encountered in many areas – estuary shallows, river and harbour mouths, wharves, rocky points and sometimes beaches.

The best equipment to fish these shallower waters is an intermediate sinking line of around 9 to 10-weight and matching rod. Use a leader of around 4-kg breaking strain. There is no need for a shock tippet, as these fish don't have much in the way of teeth, sharp scales or spines. The fish strike more readily without the shock leader too. I start with about 2 m of leader, which gives plenty of length for re-knotting and cutting back worn mono

A rocky point with a good drop-off and a nice current flowing past – an ideal spot for kahawai. Richard Dobbinson fishes in Northland's Parengarenga Harbour.

several times before having to replace the leader.

Don't worry about fishing hard on the bottom; kahawai are mostly taken either in mid-water or just under the surface when fishing from the shore. Use mid-water flies, such as deceivers or surf candies, around 8 cm long. If you get refusals, switch to smaller flies.

Berley can be a help, especially off rocks and wharves, and this may give you the opportunity to cast to sighted fish. Kahawai habitually hunt broken water, so the edges of whitewater washes are always worth prospecting.

Around river mouths, kahawai often use the hard edge of an out-flowing current against which to herd baitfish. Swinging your line across the current then strip-retrieving the fly along the edge is an effective tactic. Don't ignore the river above the mouth either – I have taken kahawai a kilometre or more up river at times. Bridges across estuaries are good choke points at which both bait and predators congregate.

On occasion, schools are visible as a dark shadow – easily mistaken for cloud shadow – off a river mouth or along a sand beach. Polaroid sunglasses are a good aid for spotting these fish. Mullet also school in this fashion, and if you are getting your fly out to the fish but are getting no strikes, this may be the problem.

Along sandy beaches, assuming there is a fairly clean bottom, fish a weighted fly along the bottom. Use an intermediate sinking line, or, if you have more depth, a weight-forward or deep-sinking shooting head. This will get your line under the surface quickly, making it less susceptible to being thrown up in a heap by waves.

Visiting Aussie fly rodder Dean Butler is delighted with this chunky Hauraki Gulf kahawai.

As is usual with beach fishing, you must pick your area. Fish tend to feed and travel along deeper-water gutters that run along the beach, fed and drained by channels that connect them back to the depths further out. These can be identified by the darker colour of the water, and a drop in wave height, or a lack of wave break over them. These are the places to fish, but they are also the most dangerous pieces of water. Take extreme care when wading.

This type of fishing often involves getting wet, so the summer months are best, and your tackle will need full washing with fresh water after such a session. To control your fly line and avoid it getting tangled by washing around in the waves, a shooting basket is a useful accessory. Be sure there are plenty of drain holes in the bottom. This beach-combing style of fishing will also turn up other species of fish, such as trevally and gurnard.

Surface schools

Schools of feeding kahawai, visible as rippling or foaming acres of surface water, used to be a common sight in most parts of the country, but have been sadly diminished by the depredations of the purse-seiners. Smaller, more scattered schools can still be encountered in most regions, however, and are an exciting fly-rod prospect.

There is something about delivering a fly into a massed school of fish – the near certainty of a strike, the mind filled with two words: 'CAN'T MISS!' This is not always the case, of course – it depends on the mood of the fish. Surface schools may be working on baitfish, such as anchovies, pilchards, yellow-eye mullet, whitebait or many others. In this case a streamer fly of the approximate size of the baitfish will hook all the fish you want. A 6 to 10-cm-long deceiver or surf candy in white and green or white and blue is ideal.

Often, however, these fish will be 'krilling': feeding on krill or other planktonic organisms. They usually work in a more orderly fashion than when feeding on baitfish, their noses bulging the surface, and rippling the surface rather than splashing it.

When kahawai are krilling, they will still often take a streamer fly, but not always. Sometimes they get really locked into selective feeding and it may be necessary to use a small shrimp pattern (pale pink or chartreuse is usually good) or small glow bug.

Krilling kahawai will often be found mixed with, or swimming just under, trevally in the northern half of the North Island. Krilling trevally can be more difficult to catch than kahawai, and a fly cast to a mixed school will often take more kahawai than trevally.

Intermediate-sinking fly lines are useful for fishing these schools, but weight-forward sinkers and shooting heads are still quite usable.

Kahawai fishing is at its most exciting when the fish are feeding in tight surface schools.

A glass-calm sea, a fly rod and a berley trail full of kahawai – perfect!

A deeply sunken fly, like a Clouser's minnow, will take bottom-feeding kahawai.

Surface schools will sometimes pass within range of shore fishermen but are mostly fished from boats. Fish can be quite nervous when in this feeding mode, and are easily spooked if you motor right up to them, sounding with a roar of white water.

The best approach is to determine their direction of feeding and position the boat upwind/up-drift of them. Turn off the engine and let the boat drift down on the school as it feeds towards you. Sometimes they will feed right up to the boat, allowing easy casting. If the fish are feeding in a relatively restricted area, you can anchor and take passing shots at the school.

When taking small or even larval baitfish, kahawai will sometimes feed in loose aggregations – individual fish feeding over a wide area, rather than tightly packed schools. This can be exciting and challenging fishing: the kahawai may be visible on the surface or from their feeding splashes, and quick accurate casts are often rewarded. I had great fun one afternoon in a small dinghy off Spirits Bay, when glass-calm conditions made cruising kahawai obvious by their bow waves, allowing sight casting to individual fish.

Berley and chunking

Kahawai respond well to berley; too well, some snapper fishermen would argue. Get a good berley trail going in a reasonable current that runs through a reefy area or past a rocky point, and the kahawai will normally turn up. Supplement minced berley with chunks of cubed pilchards or similar, and hook-ups normally come freely on small streamer flies fished through the trail with a moderate retrieve. This can sometimes be fish-a-cast action, but if the strikes stop coming, try a smaller fly and a change of colour.

Sometimes kahawai will feed deep in berley trails, or will feed on the bottom, foraging for whatever they can find. If there is no action on the surface, it pays to prospect the depths with a deep-sinking line and a weighted fly such as a Clouser's minnow. Such a rig will probe right through the water column and can then be retrieved along the bottom. This approach may yield many other species of fish in addition to kahawai. The angler should be prepared for a take at any stage – the fly is often hit on the sink!

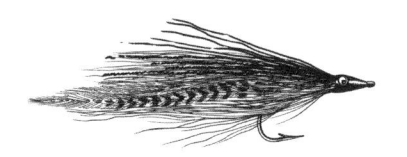

9
Targeting trevally

Trevally are one of my favourite fly-rod fish. Again, a species hammered by purse-seiners when surface schooling, their numbers have been greatly thinned out from the days when you could find them by the shimmering acre after acre, krilling on the surface in the Bay of Plenty and right through the north. Now, small surface schools are mostly found over shallower foul where purse-seiners cannot operate.

In some ways their feeding patterns are similar to kahawai, but they are often more difficult to capture. Trevally can be moody and fickle in their feeding, sometimes grabbing relatively large streamer flies freely right at the back of a boat. At other times you will find a school of surface feeders that will refuse all but the most subtle offerings.

They are dirty fighters too, like their cousins the kingfish, often heading straight for the kelp when hooked in shallow water. Turning their broad flanks to the angler, they offer powerful resistance to the end. Finally extracted from the water, their yellow fins and broad silver-opalescent sides impress, with yellow-green backs for the reef dwellers, and grey-blue for those with a more pelagic bent. Finally, they are a good table fish, with firm, flaky flesh and a good flavour.

Trevally on top

Like kahawai, surface schools of trevally get locked into selective feeding. When they are surface sipping, with those big foreheads breaking the water and vacuum-cleaner mouths sucking down tiny planktonic life, they can be difficult to approach, and difficult to persuade to take a fly. When trevally are feeding this way we often say they are krilling, but it is usually not true krill – a type of red shrimp about 50 mm long – that they are taking.

I have caught trevally on bait and jig as far south as Nelson, and know that they straggle further south than this, but have not seen them in surface schools any further south than Gisborne.

Fish feeding in this way are usually approached by boat, but there are occasions when they will come within range of rock fishermen. As with kahawai, the best way to get at these fish by boat is to motor upwind or up-current of the fish, shut down the motor and drift down onto them, hoping that they continue to feed in your direction. Some fish are easier to approach than others. The resident schools at Cape Brett in the Bay of Islands,

A selection of useful flies for trevally, depending on their mood. Top (L – R): teaser fly, berley fly, half pilchard (Pat Swift); second row (L – R): surf candy, super shrimp; third row: Clouser's minnow; forth row: deceiver.

for example, see so much tourist boat traffic that the sound of engines, and proximity of boats, does not easily put them off feeding. They are a bit like Hauraki Gulf snapper: if they stopped feeding every time a boat went past, they would starve to death!

Very occasionally you will find a co-operative surface school of trevally that will take streamer flies consistently. On other occasions you will catch one or two. There is a mug in every school, but mostly there are several keys you must use to unlock success.

Firstly, your leader will have to pass muster with the trevally's eyesight, which is fairly good in well-lit surface waters. Use clear leaders of no more than 4 – 6 kg, and no shock tippet. Go lighter if you are getting refusals.

It is a very noticeable trend that surface-feeding trevally are much easier

Small glow bugs can be a useful fly for surface-feeding trevally.

to hook late in the afternoon and first thing in the morning. By 10 am, they are getting very hard to hook. This, I am fairly sure, is because the increasing amount of light penetrating the surface makes your leader more and more obvious.

It certainly can be an advantage at times to have the ability to throw a reasonable length of cast; being able to stretch out that little bit further to a spooky school can make the difference. Use a medium-sinking line, and a 2-m leader. A 10-weight rod is a useful size for average-sized trevally.

Try not to lay your line over the school as this will often spook them, and they will sound with a crash and a splash. Rather, deliver the fly just in front of the leading edge of the school, or place just the leader and fly into them.

The right fly is important too. As the light gets up, the trevally seem to get more and more picky. Smaller sizes, and more subtle patterns, are required. Small shrimp patterns in clear, pink or chartreuse are a good starting point.

Small glow bugs in various colours sometimes work, as do teaser flies – a fly with an ice-chenille body and a short tail and hackle of matching hen feather. Red setter trout flies have sometimes proved effective too. If the trevally are on larval fish, whitebait imitations, such as tiny surf candies, can work.

At the change of light trevally become less leader shy. Richard Dobbinson took this Three Kings fish on a 10-kg tippet at dusk.

I fished a saltwater fly tournament at the Poor Knights Islands a few years ago (before it was closed to fishing) when small chartreuse flies were the key to the local trevally schools; the pattern did not seem to matter. This colour has not always proved to be a silver bullet in other areas, however.

Conventional wisdom, when faced with difficult fish, is to use longer, lighter leaders, and smaller, more subtle flies. Unfortunately, lighter leaders mean less control over the powerful, often dirty-fighting trevally, and smaller flies with lesser gaps mean a less secure hold and more pulled hooks on these soft-mouthed fish.

With small flies cast a reasonable distance to schooling fish, it is near impossible to see the take. My approach is to keep the rod tip reasonably high, and take in line at just enough pace to maintain contact with the fly. Strike at any pause or bump. Sometimes, given the density of fish, you will foul-hook one. This will make for a tough fight, although the hook will often pull out of these thin-skinned fish.

For all the perverse behaviour of surface-feeding trevally, casting a fly into such a packed school of feeding fish is one of the most exciting moments of fly fishing.

Berley trail fish

Trevally can be real berley hogs at times, and will come right up to the back of a boat, or into berley trails run when rock fishing. The berley wants to have some reasonable lumps in it – chopped up pilchards are good, and I have had some of my best results cubing or chunking with skipjack tuna cut into about 10-mm square pieces. These are fed into the water, several at a time, at regular intervals.

When the trevally start feeding on these, dead-drift a berley fly, such as a glow bug or half-pilchard fly, back to the fish, which take it as just another piece of berley.

Over the years I have had shots at my biggest trevally fishing this way – big old hump-headed cruisers of 4, 5, or 6 or more kg. Many of these monsters have dragged my line into the kelp and busted me off. I have sometimes had to use light leaders to get a take, and then found myself with a lack of firepower when trying to turn one of these powerful fish.

One technique that trevally seem to react well to is the same as that which I find

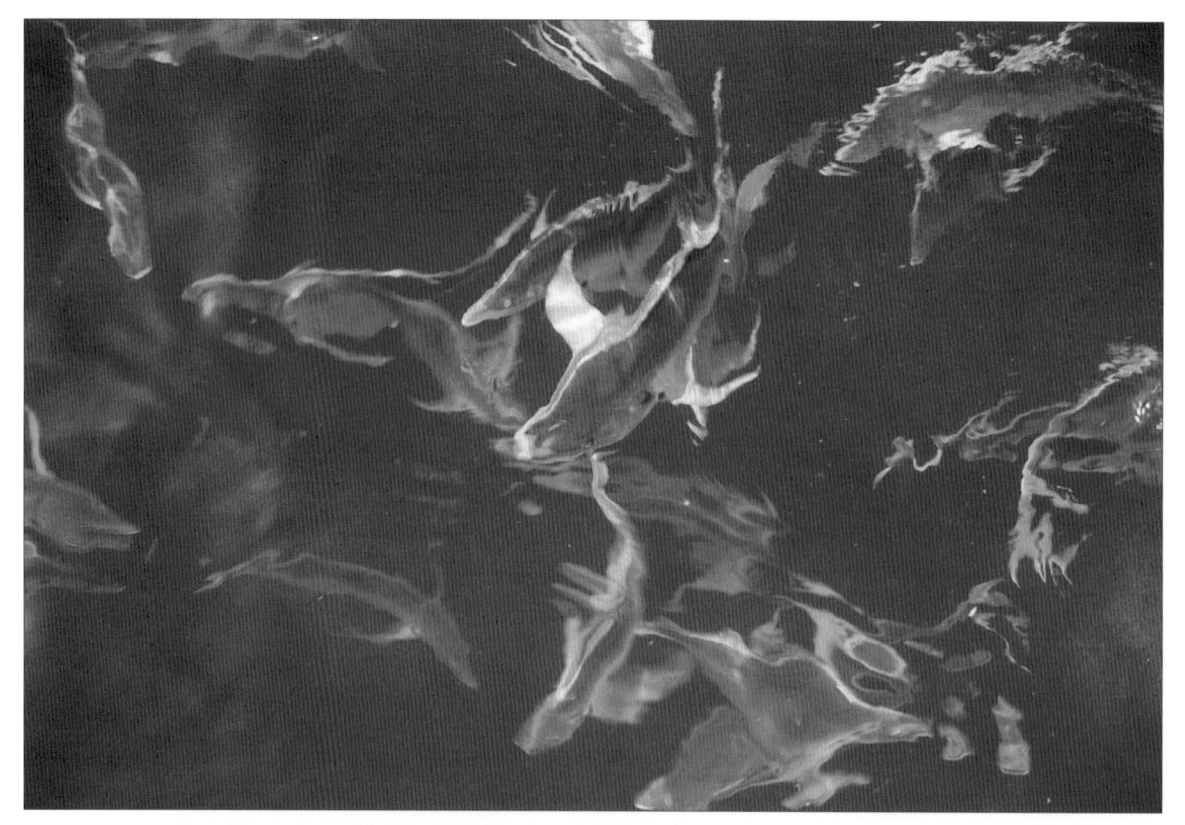

Trevally can be real berley hogs. These big White Island fish were encouraged to feed right at the transom of *Pursuit* with a berley trail of chopped pilchards, then targeted on fly.

successful on kingfish and their tropical cousins, the giant trevally: don't lean on them too hard. Playing trevally on a light drag will often be successful; maximum pressure will panic them into diving into the weeds, breaking the leader.

On occasions, particularly with the huge White Island trevally, the fish will get so excited by the berley that they will take flies on 10-kg leaders without hesitation. Then it is a toss-up as to whether maximum pressure or the softly-softly approach is best.

An evening session at the Three Kings Islands one time showed interesting responses from the trevally. I started a cube trail which soon attracted mega maomao and some trevally that looked like coffee tables with fins, swimming around on their sides. With a 4-kg leader and 10-weight rod, I was having it all my own way at first, getting plenty of hook-ups, mostly getting wiped out, but boating the odd fish to 3.5 kg. My buddies, Pat Swift and Richard Dobbinson, were using 13-weight rods and 10-kg leaders, which were being initially refused by the big trevs. However, as the last of the light went, and we could only just discern the fish as they fed like insubstantial ghosts in the cube trail, the heavy leaders became harder to see and the heavy tackle started hooking fish.

Kydd Pollock took this lumpy trevally on a 10-kg tippet and big streamer fly at White Island – a New Zealand record.

Pat and Richard caught several huge trevally, having the gear to handle them – just. The best fish was easily in excess of 6 kg – a certain New Zealand record if Pat had kept it, but it and the others were returned, as this was only the first day of a five-day stay-away.

In low-light situations the trevally seem to be less able to see the heavier leaders, just as happens with surface-feeding schools mentioned earlier. Fishing early and late for these big fish with heavier tackle may be a useful tactic if they will not play ball during the day.

Fishing for deep trevally

Trevally will not always show themselves in a berley trail, but will sometimes sit deep down and further back in the trail, particularly when the berley is finely ground and without chunks in it. This is the time when prospecting with a fast-sinking line and a weighted fly, like a Clouser's minnow, can produce the goods with trevally, as well as other species like kahawai and snapper.

Use the 'countdown' technique: this is where you slowly count as the line sinks. This will give you a depth indication that you can come back to. If the fly touches the bottom on the retrieve after you have counted to, say, twenty while the line sunk, you know if you count to eighteen or nineteen next time, you will be retrieving just above the bottom. Use a slow, jerky retrieve, letting the fly dart forward, then sink back a little.

Trevally caught this way are often only just above the bottom when hooked, and if there is a lot of weed or heavy foul, you must be very firm with them or it is all over.

In one session at Little Barrier Island in the Hauraki Gulf, I caught ten trevally and a snapper in fifteen casts. The only way I could keep the trevally from the weeds was to take a couple of quick wraps of the line around my hand (as when taking the leader on a marlin), and haul hard on the fish. This meant several bust-offs and bent fly hooks, but I got most of the fish out. Mind you, they were all around a kilo and a half, and if they had been much bigger than this, such brutal tactics would not have worked with a 4-kg tippet.

Beach and estuary

Trevally will penetrate estuaries and may sometimes be caught in quite shallow water. It would be nice to equate this with traditional 'flats' fishing found in areas such as Florida, and the Bahamas, but it is seldom possible to consistently 'sight-fish' – spot fish first and cast to them – in our estuaries. Most often, estuary fishing requires prospecting of likely spots, such as holes, junctions, flats (particularly those covered in eel grass), and man-made structures such as wharf pilings and bridges, which are also 'choke points' for travelling fish. A medium-sinking line and a general prospecting fly, such as the ubiquitous Clouser's minnow, shrimp fly or a small deceiver, are useful equipment.

Such tackle is also useful for fish that feed along beaches on the sand behind the surf line. The techniques previously described for beach-fishing kahawai will also turn up trevally (along with gurnard and other species).

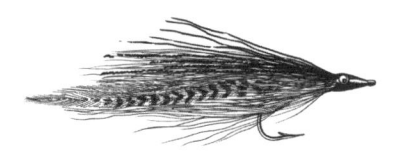

10
The challenge of snapper

Taking snapper on flies has always been a challenge, and although it is over fifteen years since I first achieved this and I now catch them regularly, I am the first to admit that I only have partial answers for taking these fish on fly.

There is much that can be adapted to fly fishing for snapper from the conventional methods of fishing for this species. For example, snapper will take jigs readily, so it stands to reason that they will also accept a fly quite happily – provided you can present it to them. Snapper will rise up off the bottom to take a sinking straylined bait, and they do the same thing with a sinking fly. A large proportion of the snapper I have caught on fly

An early fly-rod snapper. At this stage a couple of split shot on the tippet were used to get the fly down to the fish.

Pat Swift with a typical fly-caught snapper from the Bay of Islands. The big ones are harder to hook.

have nailed the fly while it was sinking. Smaller specimens of snapper seem more disposed to taking jigs, and this is true of flies too. Finally, just as berley trails can be a key to catching snapper on baits, so can berley be important to fly-rod success.

A good rock platform dropping away into deeper water and a berley trail will give the shore-based angler the opportunity to catch snapper on fly, and I have caught a number blind casting along estuarine edges where there is a good drop-off.

My initial attempts at targeting snapper on flies involved using slow-sinking flies in a berley trail. I caught a handful of snapper this way, but it was a long time between drinks. One of the important principles of straylining for snapper with baits is to use enough (but only just enough) weight to get the bait down to the snapper which are mostly on or just above the bottom. I started adding a couple of big split shot above the white deceiver flies that I was mostly using. The snapper catch rate increased noticeably.

Fly right

In about 1987 Aussie SWF guru Rod Harrison gave me a couple of prototype Clouser's minnows, then still on the 'secret weapons' list. These flies, with their built-in weighting and hook-point-up attitude, proved to be ideal for snapper, getting deep and snagging less. They have remained a firm favourite ever since. This pattern is a general purpose one – given a strip retrieve, it can imitate a baitfish, and while hopped across the bottom, it

The challenge of snapper

Clouser's minnow – probably the most consistent snapper fly.

has a crustacean-like appearance. Snapper, being broad-niche feeders, will exploit most food sources.

Successful colours have been all-white, white and green, white and chartreuse, white and red, white and pink, and just at the change of light a Clouser's that incorporates a few strips of luminous material in the body or wing is useful. A second successful pattern is a berley fly dead-drifted in the berley.

Making sure that the flies are right down in the strike zone – on the bottom – has been an important factor in targeting snapper on flies, and using weighted flies that will sink at the same sort of speed as the fly line is more effective than having a fly that lags well behind the line.

Deep-sinking fly lines are an important part of this equation, either shooting heads or weight-forward lines. If you are dealing with a current, either from an anchored boat or from the rocks, a useful tactic is to cast across and up-current so that the line and fly can sink more quickly as it drifts down-current. This is similar to the way a fly fisher may fish a wet fly in a heavy river such as the Tongariro.

The eyes have it

Looking at the position of a fish's eyes in its head is often a useful indicator as to how it feeds. A snapper's eyes allow it to look forward and up particularly well – they are

Deeply sunken flies in a berley trail produce most snapper. A double hook-up for Pat Swift and Richard Dobbinson at Waiwiri rock.

particularly aware of things coming down from above. This is one reason why they may often be found feeding on the fall-out below a working surface school of fish like kahawai – a classic jig-fishing scenario. It is also why straylined baits are so effective, mostly taken before they touch down on the bottom.

Snapper will also frequently nail flies as they sink through the water column. Several times over the years I have almost been embarrassed when I have momentarily put down a fly rod as the line was sinking to deal with some small task, only to have to dive and grab it to prevent it going over the side when a snapper has slammed the sinking fly! The lesson is always to concentrate on your gear and be prepared for a hit during every second that the fly is in the water.

Jigging flies

A technique that can work in situations from both drifting and anchored boats, where there is not too much current or wind, is almost akin to jigging. Using a deep-sinking fly line and weighted fly, cast up-current and strip whatever extra line is required into the water. You need to know the depth of the water, and have a good idea how much line you have out. This can be estimated (plus or minus) from the length of fly line.

The idea is to have your fly fairly much directly beneath you, just above the bottom, and jig it vertically up and down by stripping in a couple of metres of fly line, then dropping it back, similar to the standard jigging technique with metal lures and conventional tackle. This is much more difficult to achieve with fly tackle and is not possible to do if there is too much current or wind. It requires the right tackle, and is seldom workable in water much more than 20 m deep. But it does work. Note that there is an IGFA regulation governing the amount of line that can be stripped off the reel: 36.57 m (120 ft).

Targeting the big ones

Although I have caught well in excess of fifty snapper on fly, I have never managed one much bigger than a couple of kilos. Is this just happenstance (there being a great many more small snapper out there than big ones), or do the big ones require a new tactic?

As snapper get bigger and older, they seem to get more piscivorous – they hunt and eat fish. This falls back to the energy equation: they must get more energy out of what they eat than they expend in catching it or they start to lose condition, hunting efficiency, and will ultimately starve. Small livebaits are an effective way to target large snapper.

Translating this across to SWF, it may be that larger flies, 10 to 15 cm long, may be the way to target larger snapper. Also important, of course, is to fish where the big ones are. If you fish where the schoolies are, that is what you will catch. Big fish will congregate in certain areas (at least in northern waters) in spring just prior to and during spawning. They can be quite aggressive at this time and this is probably the best opportunity to target them.

Finally, the change of light is

Visiting American angler Joel Kalman (R) took this huge snapper from Murray Nicholls' *Waimana* **in April 1999. At 13.38 kg – just a shade under 30 old-fashioned pounds – it is a 4-kg tippet world record that will probably stand for a long, long time.** Photo: Murray Nicholls

usually the best time to fish for snapper, with the bigger fish coming on the bite at this time. A big fly with some luminous material in its make-up fished at this time is a good tactic.

There is still plenty of scope for experimentation in the field of fly fishing for snapper, but they now represent a regular target species for the fly rodder.

A luminous-bodied Clouser's minnow fished at the change of light was the undoing of this Waitemata Harbour snapper.

Above: Jock stewarts, or scarpies, are a regular catch when prospecting southern waters with flies.
Below: Yellowfin and skipjack attack a meatball of baitfish off Whakatane. This is a prime fly-rod opportunity.

Above left: A much younger author with a fly-rod snapper taken on a home-built rod and a converted Olympic fly reel. There was no SWF tackle commercially available in NZ in the early 1980s.

Above right: Breaking new ground: (L – R) 'Bonze' Fleet, Skipper Bruce Martin, Mike Brown, and the author with New Zealand's first SWF marlin.

Below: A skipjack tuna taken fly casting around a meatball from *Pursuit* off Whakatane. After showing the author his spool knot twice, it weighed in at 5.17 kg and became the world record on 4-kg tippet.

Above: Pat Swift (L) and Mark Kitteridge in fly-fishing paradise among the obliging schools of trevally and kahawai at Cape Brett.
Below: This huge berley-trail trevally was caught by Pat Swift on a cube fly at the Three Kings.

Above: Meatball action off Whakatane can mean a great opportunity at several species of tuna. Getting a scoop of baitfish out of the meatball is an important part of the equation.
Below: Mark Kitteridge with one of a nice catch of tarakihi taken on small Clouser's minnows from a berley trail in the Bay of Islands one evening.

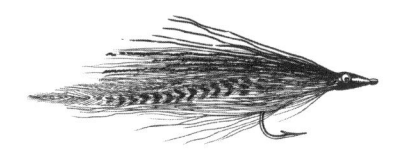

11
Chasing kingfish

Kingfish would have to rank among the top flight of fly-rod target species. Like snapper, hooking the smaller specimens is not too difficult, given the right situation, but getting onto the bigger fish is harder. Even the small ones are tough propositions to land, and given the kings' often-demonstrated habit of diving for cover when hooked, catching a decent-sized fish on a fly rod is a real challenge.

The gear

Rods in the 9 to 10-weight range are fine on 'rat' kings, but anything over, say, 5 kg is better suited to a 10 – 12 weight. For the big boys, the lifting power of a 12 – 14 weight

Kingfish are powerful, dirty fighters and one of the toughest fly-rod opponents.

distinct advantage. I like a reel that will hold at least 300 m of 15-kg backing.

Tippets ranging from 6 kg to 10 kg are fine for kingfish, in conjunction with 300 mm of 20-kg shock leader, mostly to cope with line abrasion around the mouth. If you are not worried about fishing to IGFA regulations, you might want to push your tippet up to 15 kg. However, there is no point in going any higher than this, as you will snap your fly line or backing before the tippet, and fly lines are not cheap!

Flies for kingfish

Flies have an advantage over many other types of lures used on kings, in that the fish will take them at quite slow speeds, so the subsonic retrieve often needed to turn on kings to metal jigs is not required.

Kingfish like flies of reasonable size, and I have had good success with the deceiver pattern, between 100 and 150 mm in length. Hooks should be strong, forged-shank models. A good colour is basic white, often with some counter-shading of blue, green or whatever on the top of the wing. These flies have a great swimming action, and seem to be particularly enticing to kings.

Another successful fly, particularly in high current areas, is a large Clouser's minnow tied with flash material and extra weight in the body.

On one occasion, when all else failed, I had success with a difficult king by using a popping fly. The easiest way to have this option available, as mentioned in Chapter 5, is to make a few cup-shaped popping heads out of cork, polystyrene or packing foam, and put a hole through the middle with a hot wire. These can be used in conjunction with a conventional fly by sliding them down the leader to sit at the top of the fly.

When using popping flies, a floating or slow-sinking fly line is used, so that a belly does not develop between the rod tip and the fly. This can make it very difficult to set the hook into the fish. The other down side to floating flies is that the bow wave pushed by the attacking fish can sometimes push the buoyant fly out of the way, resulting in a missed strike.

Let us run through a few typical situations and methods for taking kings on the fly.

Kingfish like flies with some bulk. Shown here (top to bottom) are a deceiver, piper fly, surf candy, popping head on a Harlens streamer fly, and, at right, a super-flash Clouser's minnow.

This 7-kg king took a streamer fly fished in a berley trail at the Bay of Islands. It was a tough fight on a 6-kg tippet.

Schooling fish

Rat kings are often found in conjunction with surface-schooling fish like trevally and kahawai, mostly swimming underneath them. To get through the surface school to the kings underneath is easiest with trevally. A big fly, which kahawai would grab, is generally ignored by the trevs, allowing it to sink through them and down to the kings.

When fishing from a boat, a reasonable degree of casting ability is required, as trevally will often sound if you get too close, taking the kings with them. A shooting head or weight-forward line is favoured for distance casting with a heavy, bulky fly. Getting up-current of the school, and drifting down with the engine off, is the best way to approach. Cast to the leading edge of the school and retrieve the fly fairly rapidly, in metre-long strips.

Berley trails

Kings are susceptible to berley trails, particularly ones with pilchards or cubes of oily fish, like skipjack. This method works equally well off the rocks or out of a boat. Opotiki-based fishing guide Mark Draper has made a speciality of SWF off the rocks and has produced some big kingfish for his clients, including the current world record on 10-kg tippet. Often you will see the fish, but this is not always the case. Fishing a sunken fly blind in a berley trail will often produce fish, both kings and many other species.

Berley off the rocks attracted this king to where Stephane Uzan could cast to it. At 25.20 kg it became the 10-kg tippet world record. A feather in the cap of Opotiki-based guide Mark Draper, who has engineered some great kingfish catches for his clients. Photo: Mark Draper

If you are fishing from an anchored boat in a likely area (over a reef, near a point, outside a harbour entrance), it is best to have a buoy attached to the anchor so that it can be ditched quickly if you need to follow a hooked fish.

Follow the leader

Kings have a habit of hanging out in schools, and when one fish is hooked, say on a jig or bait, its mates will often follow it up to the boat. An angler ready and waiting with a fly rod when a fish is brought up will often get a shot in this situation.

It takes a bit of discipline to wait with a fly rod for something that may or may not happen, while people around you are hooking up on conventional gear. When you get that hook-up, however, it is all worthwhile.

FADs

FAD is an acronym for Fish Aggregation Device. These are usually buoys or rafts anchored in an area where they attract pelagic species, particularly tuna, so that they may be more easily located and caught. This takes advantage of the fascination of pelagic species with floating objects.

Initially, this attraction was explained by small fish taking shelter around the structure, and larger fish being attracted to feed on them. While this may be partly the case, the relatively small amount of bait is not sufficient to support the huge amount of predators sometimes found in the vicinity of a FAD. Sonic tagging experiments have shown that predatory fish may roam 10 km from a FAD, but return to it periodically, using it as a sort of a base.

These devices are occasionally deployed in New Zealand waters, but we have plenty of

Aussie fly-rod guru Rod Harrison unrolls a long cast to kingfish holding around 'A' buoy in Auckland's Rangitoto Channel.

Channel marker buoys, like this one, act as floating kingfish attractors in northern waters.

natural structures, and FADs don't seem to last long before storms or passing ships wipe them out. The New Zealand frigate *Te Kaha* wrapped one of the Tongan FADs around its prop in the late '90s – that one was kept pretty quiet.

Kingfish in particular are attracted to floating objects, both constructed and natural, and may well use them as an ambush point for attacking passing baitfish. Anything floating is worth checking out for kingfish. Channel marker buoys are well-known holders of kings, and those in Auckland and Whangarei Harbours get plenty of attention from local anglers.

I once took visiting Australian fishing journalists Rod Harrison and Dave Harrigan (then editor of *Australian Fishing World* magazine) out to 'A' Buoy in Auckland's Rangitoto Channel. The kings were in residence, and Rod, great fly fisherman that he is, soon had a good one hooked on the fly. He was unfortunately wearing a pair of track-suit pants with dodgy elastic, and with Dave and I both perched in the bow of the 5-m tinny with cameras at the ready, Rod had the choice of using both hands to keep the king out of the buoy's anchor chain or preserving his modesty by holding up his strides. Modesty won and the king made it to the chain!

Boats that have been on their moorings for a long time will collect fish too. I pulled some fly-rod kings from under a long-time moored launch in Houhora Harbour once, and a Russian freighter, under arrest in the Hauraki Gulf for eighteen months, became a massive FAD with a metre of marine growth underneath and its own resident school of kingfish.

Floating logs often hold kingfish too. I pulled a number of kings, kahawai and barracouta from under a log off Napier once on conventional tackle, and the timber that bobbed around off the Bay of Plenty after Cyclone Bola for about six months held big numbers of kings.

There are times when everything comes together to make a perfect fishing memory. One of these occurred for me off White Island a few years ago, on Rick Pollock's boat, *Pursuit* (the first one). We were jigging and casting to schools of surface trevally, maomao and rat kings, and I was up on the bow with a fly rod and baitcaster.

I was playing a rat king on the baitcaster, as we drifted down on a school. The school was about 25 m out, and I could see the kings under the trevally. It was too much. I passed the king on the baitcaster to the deckie to finish off, and grabbed the fly rod – a 9 to 10-weight with a 6-kg tippet.

It was one of those casts that make up for half-a-dozen fluffed ones. The shooting head rocketed out, and the shooting line, which had been lying in a pile on the deck and had every excuse to be tangled, followed without a hitch. The leader uncurled perfectly and dropped the fly right at the leading edge of the school.

There was an initial flurry as a handful of spooked trevally made way for the fly. I let it sink for a few seconds, then began to retrieve the fly. On the second strip, a king crashed the fly and I was on.

I had fifteen minutes of hard fight to get it to the boat, where the fly was removed, and the fish released. It was only a small fish, around 5 kg, but the circumstances of its capture gave me more satisfaction than a fish four times its size would have done on conventional tackle. Saltwater fly fishing does that to you.

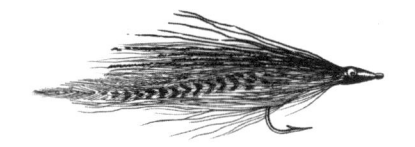

12
Barracouta and warehou

These two species may seem like odd bedfellows, but they are both cooler-water fish that may be found at any level in the water column, often close to the surface.

Warehou

Warehou are relatives of the deep-water bluenose. They are more common in the southern part of their range, the east coast of the South Island, but straggle as far north as the Bay of Plenty when the water is at its coldest. In years past David Graham in his classic book, *Treasury of New Zealand Fishes,* mentions big concentrations of these fish in

Wellington angler Keith Michael works a fish in perfect weather on Hunter's Bank.

shallow water inside the Otago heads and Oamaru Harbour, but they were heavily purse-seined and seemed to have been pretty well wiped out in the 1930s.

These days, their most reliable appearance is in midwinter in the Cook Strait-Wellington region, where they are targeted by recreational fishermen with both conventional and fly gear. Well-known local charter operator Pete Lamb reports that the main schools of these fish appear around June – July in water temperatures of around 12º C, a situation matching nicely with a hot warehou jigging session I once had at Steven's Passage in the Marlborough Sounds. The schools stay through the spring, with a few stragglers sometimes hanging on into November. However, not every year is a good warehou year.

These Cook Strait fish are gravid and close to spawning. They spread out over reefs and structures in the Cook Strait area, with such spots as Fisherman's Rock and Hunter's Bank well known, but many other reefs also produce the goods, including those on the Marlborough Sounds side.

Warehou feed on worms, crabs, shrimp and shellfish on the bottom, small baitfish such as pilchards, and particularly true krill in mid-water. These red-orange coloured crustaceans are around 5 – 7 cm in length, and it is worth noting that bait fly rigs with red dressing on the hooks are particularly successful.

A weighted fly is a good option to get at subsurface and mid-water schools, and the good old Clouser's minnow tied in a combination of red, orange and pink would be hard to beat.

Check out likely reefs with a sounder, looking for mid-water sign, particularly on the up-current faces of structures – this is one of fishing's universal rules of thumb. Starting up-current of the sign, drift through it, using weighted flies and fast-sinking lines to get down to the fish.

Keith Michael took this fly-rod warehou from a school off the Kapiti Coast.
Photo: Keith Michael

Warehou grow to about 6 kg and are strong performers. They are clean fighters (although I once lost one that took my line around a commercial dropper line at Fisherman's Rock), and can be taken on 9 to 10-weight gear and 6-kg leaders.

Barracouta

Many mainstream fishermen consider barracouta to be the scum of the seven seas (all right, the Pacific and the Tasman, but 'scum of the two seas' doesn't sound anywhere near as good), and I once wrote a piece about how to avoid catching them on conventional tackle.

Only tackle dealers love them, and a sports-store owner I know was once seen gently and jokingly wrapping one in a wet towel, carefully unhooking it, then touching up the edges of its teeth with a hook stone before slipping it back over the side!

SWF anglers look at things from a slightly different point of view, however. The fishing is done largely for the sheer fun of it, and any fish on a fly is a good fish. Looking at them without bias, 'couta are handsome enough in their iridescent chrome-purple-blue. The degree of fight varies from fish to fish. Some will fight hard enough to convince you that you have a nice snapper or a small kingfish, and on a 9 to 10-weight rod just about any 'couta will give a reasonable fight. You can go right down in rod weight and tippet strength if you want more of a challenge.

Although the spiritual home of the barracouta is in the deep south, they seem to be getting more numerous and spreading further north as the years pass. This is one species where the commercial sector nowhere near approaches their total allowable catch. It seems that as species like kahawai are thinned out by commercial fishing, the barracouta expand to fill the niche.

What this boils down to is a lot of opportunities for the fly fisher. In the far south and the southern half of the North Island, barracouta are common all year round. In the northern half of the North Island, these fish are thick during the winter months but seem to withdraw further south as the water heats up.

In the northern winter it is enough to go to any snapper reef and start berleying to have all the barracouta you can catch under the boat. Off Dunedin I have seen them in frothing, slashing surface schools, almost as far as the eye can see. When these guys really get going, they hit anything in the water. In a situation like this it is sometimes a good idea to give the fishing a miss – severe damage to, or total loss of your fly line can result.

Shock leader

In a less out-of-control situation, your shock tippet (in this case more correctly termed 'bite leader') will give sufficient protection from the mouthful of fangs these fish sport. Any light wire will do the job. I usually use Halco Lockweld Wire, which is secured

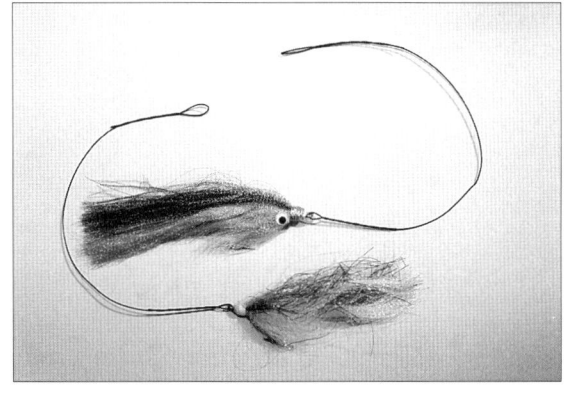

A couple of sacrificial 'couta flies fitted with Lockweld plastic-coated wire shock tippets.

Through a fly-rodder's eyes, barracouta can be a fun fish to catch.

by twisting together then fusing the nylon coating with a flame. I like it because it is easy to use, and the outer nylon coating allows me to tie my mono leader direct to the wire with an albright knot.

Other materials may also serve well. One day in Fiordland I caught five barracouta on a single shock leader of 24-kg fluorocarbon without any apparent damage. Another new material which I have recently received for testing is called Knottable Steel Trace. This is a stainless steel outer mesh with a spectra inner. It is supple, knottable and should join direct to monofilament. Being able to join the shock leader material direct to the mono leader is a bonus. If you have to use a crimp and swivel, these items will often attract the attention of the toothy ones and they will bite you off at the leader connection. Likewise, try to avoid bulky and brightly coloured whippings and splices on other line connections.

Flies for 'couta?

When they are in the mood (and this is most of the time), they will take almost anything, any size, any colour. I must admit to using discards from the tying bench and other uglies from the fly box – a good way of cleaning out those passengers you don't really like, but can't bring yourself to throw out. If I were tying a fly especially for barracouta, I would tend to reds, yellows, and lots of flash. It would need to be robust, easy to tie, and have a bit of weight to get down. I think you see where this is going – yes, another variation of the Clouser's minnow!

Another option when the 'couta are on the go are surface popping flies. They will be taken readily if worked in strips across the surface, and the surface strike adds extra excitement to proceedings. Just be sure if you are using a separate popping head on a fly, that it cannot ride up the leader during the fight where it will attract the strikes of other fish in the school, resulting in a cut-off.

The attrition rate in tackle can be high when fishing for barracouta, but with the right mental attitude, they can be considered a sportfish for the fly rodder rather than a trash fish, and can provide a whole lot of fun when the average bottom fisher would exit, swearing!

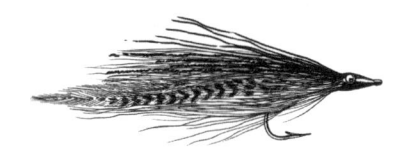

13
The bottom fish

There are a number of inshore species which are quite catchable on fly, and can be counted as legitimate fly-rod targets.

Parore

Sometimes called black snapper, and known as luderick or blackfish in parts of Australia, parore is a species not much fished for in New Zealand. There is a saying: 'If it eats fish, it will eat flies.' In the case of the largely herbivorous parore we can stretch the aphorism further – even if it doesn't eat fish, we can still sometimes catch it on flies.

But this is not quite true; we used to catch parore off the Russell wharf on tuatua baits. Their stomach contents sometimes contain the odd crab, and recently one of my fishing companions, to my surprise, caught one on a piece of pilchard. Perhaps these fish can be likened to vegetarians who feel it is OK to eat chicken, and occasionally weaken to the smell of frying bacon.

Parore can be found feeding around ocean rocks, including those offshore. They frequently enter harbours, estuaries and tidal rivers. Most common from North to East Cape, they straggle south to Cook Strait on both coasts. They feed on several types of weed, including sea lettuce, green filamentous algae, and eel grass. Areas where these weeds are well grazed down are worth checking for parore as the tide covers them. As well as natural structures, parore often may be seen grazing on the algae growing on wharf pilings and marina pontoons.

My first fly-rod encounter with parore was many years ago at Matapouri, near Tutukaka. In a stream flowing from the mangroves, across the sand and into the harbour, I could see four fish. They were feeding like trout, swaying from side to side in the current, intercepting small pieces of green algae drifting down in the current.

Hastening back to my car, I ratted through my gear and set up a 7-weight trout rod, floating line, and a shaggy green stonefly nymph which had a fair similarity to the weed on which the parore were feeding. After several presentations one of the fish took the fly, and was hooked. Its run back for the safety of deeper water would have done justice to a big Tongariro rainbow.

In Australia, fly fishermen target these fish with small flies (size 10 or 12), rough tied

Parore can be taken on green weed imitations, and may sometimes be tempted by a small berley fly.

with green imitation seal's fur. An added refinement is a small cork or neoprene strike indicator, such as those that were used for trout fishing before treated yarn took over. This suspends the fly and allows it to be fished blind around the rocks, wharf or whatever. Any unnatural movement of the strike indicator should be struck at.

Parore will respond to berley. When fishing for them with weed baits and floats, a berley of mixed sand and chopped weed is used, but occasionally they respond to a more protein-packed brew. I was fishing with keen fly rodder Richard Dobbinson near Auckland recently. We had a berley trail of minced skipjack running and had taken some nice kahawai on our flies when we noticed some fish feeding in a wash on the corner of the reef off which we were anchored. Eventually, a handful of these parore, almost guiltily it seemed, came across and started feeding on small fragments of berley behind the boat. Richard managed to get a couple of takes on a size 14 hare's ear nymph, a trout fly that resembled in texture and colour the berley sludge. Unfortunately, neither fish stuck.

A berley of chopped green sea lettuce and sand is sometimes used for parore.

Gurnard

These fish are hunters of sedimentary bottoms, feeding on small crustaceans, such as crabs and shrimps, worms and very small fish. I have caught them the length of the country on conventional tackle, including Fiordland where the tea-coloured water of the upper sounds had brought a colour change from orange, gold and silver to mud browns and blacks in this usually colourful fish.

Large harbours, such as the Kaipara and Manukau, hold a lot of gurnard, as do large sedimentary bays such as Hawke's Bay. Surfcasters and kite fishers working sandy beaches get their fair share as well, and it is probably the fly caster working a sandy beach with a moderate drop-off that has the best chance. Work the channels and gutters with a moderate-sinking line and a fly like a small Clouser's minnow or a crab imitation skipped slowly across the bottom. Sea conditions need to be settled, and moderate wading will probably be required.

Useful flies – top (L – R): commercially tied McCrab and epoxy flies (for gurnard and flatfish); second row (L – R): ice chenille berley fly and weed fly (for parore), small Clouser's minnow (for tarakihi).

A fly that is tied reversed – so that the point rides upward – will prevent a lot of snagging, and also help preserve the sharpness of the point. This is something to keep an eye on, as gurnard have hard bony plates around their mouths and require a firm strike and a sharp hook. A leader in the 4 or 6-kg class will do the job with these fish, which average under a kilo in weight.

John dory

This is another predatory fish readily available to the fly rodder. Although they are caught right out to deep water (I recently pulled one from 210 m while hapuku fishing with livebait), they are common in estuaries, around rocks and wharves, and over inshore reefs. Although they have been reported from right around the country, they are most common around the top half of the North Island.

John dory are not strong swimmers, and must hunt by stealth. I have watched them hunt many times, from wharves, rocks and while snorkelling. These thin-bodied fish, with their kelp camouflage colour scheme, approach their prey head on so as to be least noticeable. They scull gently into range with subtle movements of secondary dorsal and anal fins. If they can get close enough, they shoot out their incredible extending mouth. The vacuum formed causes an inrush of water with sweeps the prey in with it.

John dory mostly hunt small fish and shrimps, but are successful with only a small percentage of their stalks. Although a common catch on small livebaits, and a regular taker of yo-yoed jigs, john dory are less frequently taken on fly than you might expect from such a fish. I believe the reason is that the dory hunt s-l-o-w-l-y, and that the usual strip retrieve is too fast for these curious fish to get in a position to try and take the fly.

A Clouser's minnow fished slowly along the bottom hooked this john dory for Richard Dobbinson.

The answer is a very slow retrieve, and to avoid hanging up the fly on the bottom, an intermediate-sinking line, along with a slower-sinking fly (such as a small deceiver), may be preferable in shallower waters. In some situations you can see the dory feeding (or trying to feed) in shallow water, and this is an ideal situation in which to target them. Get the fly down in the vicinity of the fish and leave it there, just giving it an occasional twitch. Let the fish come to it, and don't be over-eager on the strike.

Flatfish

Various types are found in shallow water right around the country, including both flounder and sole. In practical terms it is not necessary to be able to tell them apart. They all taste good except for the left-eyed witch flounder, which is nearly solid bone. All flatfish have a minimum size of 25 cm, except for the diamond-shaped sand flounder which has a minimum of 23 cm.

Flounder seem to feed mostly on small crabs, sand hoppers, and worms. These prey items are much more common in muddy areas than nice clean sandy ones, which is a little unfortunate as it makes the fishing less pleasant. Flatfish stalk these prey items in the ultra-shallows – this, after all, is what they are designed to do.

The shore-based fly rodder can stalk these fish along estuarine fringes, sight fishing on the rising tide. Look (and listen) for splashes, ripples, mud puffs – anything that may indicate a hunting flatfish.

A 3 or 4-kg leader is plenty, and a small fly imitating a crab or worm is cast into the very shallow water where the flatfish is hunting. Let it sit and let the fish approach to within a metre or less, then give the fly a small twitch to attract the fish's attention. Let the flounder stalk the fly, while giving the fly the occasional twitch. When the flounder pounces, don't strike immediately – they seem to pin their prey with their head until they take it into their mouth in a second movement, so postpone the strike briefly.

Another scenario is blind fishing in channels or mangrove creeks in which the flatfish travel. Again, the fly wants to be very slowly twitched across the bottom.

Tarakihi

These are another fish that can be counted as a fly-rod target in the right situation. They will certainly take lures: I have caught quite a number on small metal jigs and conventional gear. Witness also the success of the 'Tarakihi Terror' bait fly string that I helped design for Black Magic Tackle. The trick is to be able to get the fly to the fish with fly-casting tackle.

Once, in a matter of about a week, I caught tarakihi on conventional tackle from out of 400 m of water in the Bay of Plenty, and out of 4 m at Stewart Island, indicating both the geographical and depth range of this sought-after table fish. The bigger tarakihi now tend to be found on deep offshore spots, although this appears to be a result of fishing pressure rather than habitat requirements. Average-sized fish seem to move onto shallower reefs during

Rick Wakelin took this flounder blind fishing a fly along the bottom of a Manukau mangrove creek.

the winter in the north, and during summer-autumn in the south, perhaps reflecting a preference for a certain water temperature. It is when they are in these shallower waters that they can be targeted by fly fishers, even those fishing off the rocks, assuming there is a reasonable drop-off into deeper water.

Tarakihi feed on crustaceans, including crabs, shrimps and krill, worms, shellfish, and small squid. Flies that imitate these types of feed work well, and added to the need to sink the fly, this suggests a small Clouser's minnow fished on a fast-sinking line.

We had a good session on SWF tarakihi several years ago in November in the Bay of Islands. Anchored in a sandy bay of medium depth for the night, we ran a berley trail to see what could be lured out of the reef at the end of the bay. As the sun dropped away, I hooked a hard-pulling fish on a small white Clouser's minnow. It resisted stoutly, but didn't take much line – a chunky tarakihi. Soon, all of the lads were into them. Mark Kitteridge had the best results on a white and blue Clouser's tied on a size 6 hook, which accounted for about half-a-dozen fish.

These species are all good table fish, although parore flesh can be tainted if the fish are not cleaned immediately after they are killed, and the black stomach lining removed from the fillets. You can get the best of both worlds – good sport and a feed on the table.

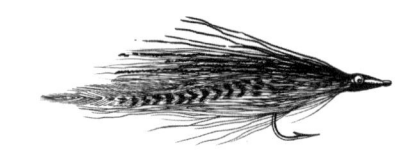

14
Deep-water techniques

There is a saying I have already quoted: 'If it eats fish, it will eat flies', meaning any predatory fish can be targeted successfully with fur-and-feather imitations of its prey. This concept can be expanded to include fish that feed on other marine organisms such as shrimps, crabs, krill and so on.

Many common inshore fish have now been captured by saltwater fly fishing, but the SWF method does have limitations. One of the greatest of these is presentation – getting the fly to the fish. In the case of deep-water species, the problem is not so much that they will not take a fly, but getting the fly down to them.

Current, the extra buoyancy inherent in salt water (compared with fresh), the relatively light weight of a fly (compared with a jig or a sinker), and the thickness of the fly line all conspire to put a practical cap of about twenty-odd metres of depth that the fly can penetrate to in most circumstances. A final limit is a new regulation from the IGFA stating that the maximum amount of line that can be stripped off the reel (by the angler, not the fish) is 120 ft (36.57 m).

Hapuku on fly?

Hapuku, or groper to those south of the Mason-Dixon line, were a target species that I had thought would take a fly if you could just get one down to them. After all, they will readily take a jig or livebait. Although many consider these fish a species of deep water only, this is not the case. It is just that they have been fished out of most shallow habitats.

There are, however, some places that hapuku can still be found in shallow water. I know of occasional inshore catches from many parts of the country. However, realistically the mid to lower Wairarapa coast is probably a reasonable bet, as is Fiordland and the Chatham Islands, where groper can be caught off the rocks in places.

As mentioned in an earlier chapter, I toted a light SWF rod to Fiordland a couple of years ago, and between fishing for bluefin tuna, did a little fly casting from shore. The fish were prolific if not big. Wading through a mass of various wrasses and jock stewarts, and oddities like butterfly perch, I managed a small trumpeter and a blue cod. None of them had the grunt to take any line. Still, the blokes I was fishing with, Fiordland crayfishermen Mark Harris and Ron Grant, could see how keen I was on SWF.

Some time later I got a call from Mark: 'Sam, next time you come down after bluefin, bring your fly rod. We have found some places where you can catch groper in about fifteen metres of water – if you can get past the trumpeter and big blue cod.'

'Sounds like a terrible place, mate,' I answered. Woo-hoo! This had to be a good bet – after many years of working the coasts of Fiordland, these blokes really know their stuff.

Time moves on like a big steam-roller, and eighteen months down the track I was getting ready for another trip to the Last Frontier. The programme was trolling for bluefin tuna, but to tell the truth, I was just as keen for the opportunity to have a crack at a hapuku on fly – and those trumpeter and blue cod I had to get past. Sitting at the fly-tying bench, I designed some flies for the task.

The fly for the job

For hapuku, a fly needs to look big, but still sink fast. I settled on Gamakatsu SL12S hooks – a wide gape, but still fairly fine in the wire and barb so they would not be too hard to set. I tied it reversed, with dumb-bell eyes on top of the fly so it would swim point up and reduce the chance of snagging. The fly had to sink well to get down to the strike zone, so I added a couple of wraps of lead wire from some old leadline to the shank, and slipped some mylar tube over the top. To give the impression of bulk, I added a dressing of broad saltwater flashabou – flashy but not dense. It would make the fly look big but not hold a lot of water (making it heavy to cast), or impede the sink rate too much. The completed fly was about 20 cm long, and tied broadly in the style of a Clouser's minnow.

As it turned out, the bluefin were near non-existent. Warm water appeared to have pushed them well south of Stewart Island, However, the sea was perfect the whole week that my buddy Carl Angus and I were aboard the *Ake Ake*, and the skies were clear – very unusual for Fiordland, and very welcome. Although the bluefin did not play ball, we caught albacore to about 17 kg on troll gear. Fiordland is just a fabulous place to be – the grandeur of the place is just stunning, especially in weather as magnificent as we encountered.

Get down

The two sessions we spent bottom fishing were the standouts. Moving in to the rugged coast, we drifted over shallow inshore reefs. Ron Grant, Mark Harris and Geoff Small took turns at berleying (with a gruesome mix of chicken guts and paua hua that is a favourite with cod potters), and working a conventional jig rod. Carl Angus stuck with baits, and I worked the fly. Our first session mostly produced blue cod, including four on the fly rod, the best of which would have bettered 3 kg.

The following day, we tried the same system on a different reef, again in

The Clouser's minnow is one of the best of the sinking flies and rides point up, reducing snagging. The large version at the top was tied especially for hapuku, but has now taken a wide range of species.

Hapuku on fly! The author took this fish and another on a deeply sunken fly in Fiordland, one of a handful of areas where they can still be found on shallow reefs.

perfect conditions. Ron pulled up a couple of hapuku on the jig, while Carl seemed to be catching mostly trumpeter on his small cut baits. I cast my fly down-drift and stripped a little extra fly line to help it sink. With no wind and little current, the fly line looked near-vertical by the time we had drifted down on it. The bottom ranged from 17 to 25 m, and my buddies had proven that the fish were there with conventional methods.

Using a 13-weight rod, I had only made a couple of strips of the retrieve when the line came up tight. I struck as hard as I dared on the 10-kg tippet, and was connected to something powerful. The heavy tail-beats pulsed through the rod tip, then the fish raced off up around the bow of the *Ake Ake*, taking me deep into the backing.

The long rod gave me some protection in terms of keeping the line off the hull, but I was facing an obstacle course of rigging and stays to get to the bow. Mark saw my problem and eased the boat ahead to put me back over the fish. Hapuku are tough fighters in shallow water, but there is a lot of grunt in those GIII 13-weight rods. After a bit of knock-down, drag-out, I got the fish off the bottom and slowly worked it to the surface.

Finally, we could see it, deep down – it was a hapuku! I was all nerves now, but Geoff made no mistake with the gaff. What a buzz – a hapuku on fly! It was a pretty fish, in top condition, and somewhere around 12 kg in weight.

Coming up trumps

The fish kept coming. Ron pulled a hapuku of around 20 kg on a jig, surviving a near spool-job on his small boat reel. Carl finally got over his trumpeter fixation when we talked him into putting on some decent-sized baits, and caught a couple of hapuku on his 8-kg rig.

Acutely aware that fly-rod opportunities like this are rare, I got the fly back in the water. Although it took a while for the fly to sink down to where the fish were, they did not hesitate to strike as soon as I began a retrieve. A couple of trumpeter in the 3 to 4-kg range fell to the fly, and then, to prove it was no fluke, a second hapuku. This was a smaller fish of around 8 kg. The dreaded barracouta also started making an appearance, and I caught four or five on fly. However, a shock tippet of 24-kg Seguar fluorocarbon offered good protection, and I didn't lose any flies, or even have to re-rig. Tough stuff.

We moved in to a shallower spot of around 10 m to see what other species of fish we could lure to the fly. I went to a 10-weight rod, 6-kg tippet and a lighter, smaller fly. First a pugnacious banded wrasse took the fly, then when we started the chicken and paua berley going, big blue cod were coming right up to the surface to feed. I caught another four on the fly, up to about 2 kg, and dropped a couple of bigger ones, then it was time to go.

Some nice Fiordland trumpeter also fell for the author's deep-water technique.

This day of saltwater fly was one of the highlights of that summer for me, and I am grateful to Mark and Ron for making it happen – a case of preparation meeting opportunity.

Although Fiordland is 'tiger country', and many fishing opportunities exist there that are not available in more heavily fished regions, this system of drifting (or even anchoring on) shallow reefs with berley and deeply sunken fly can produce a lot of fun, and access to otherwise unreachable (with a fly) fish in many parts of the country.

The main components are a fast-sinking fly line, and a weighted fly that will keep pace with the line as it sinks, not lag behind. The rest is being in the right place at the right time – where the fish are, with not too much depth or current.

Pat Swift (L) and Richard Dobbinson with a pair of golden snapper that took deep flies after dark at the Three Kings.

Cast down-drift, or, if you are anchored, cast up-current. Strip extra line into the water to allow the fly and fly line to sink more quickly (being mindful of the IGFA restriction on this mentioned earlier). You need to have a good idea of the depth of the water (from your sounder) and the amount of line out (inferred from the known length of fly line). As the boat drifts over the fly line, or as the fly line drifts past the boat if you are at anchor, the fly should be at maximum depth – in the strike zone with time enough to make some short strip retrieves, and maybe a couple of drop-backs, before the whole thing must be retrieved and re-cast.

This is a similar technique to deep-water jigging with flies, mentioned in Chapter 10. Obviously, this method has application right through the country, not just in southern waters. A recent SWF trip to the Three Kings Islands saw us using this technique in the evening at the anchorage. We accounted for a long string of golden snapper, pink maomao, blue cod, and even a hard-running eagle ray!

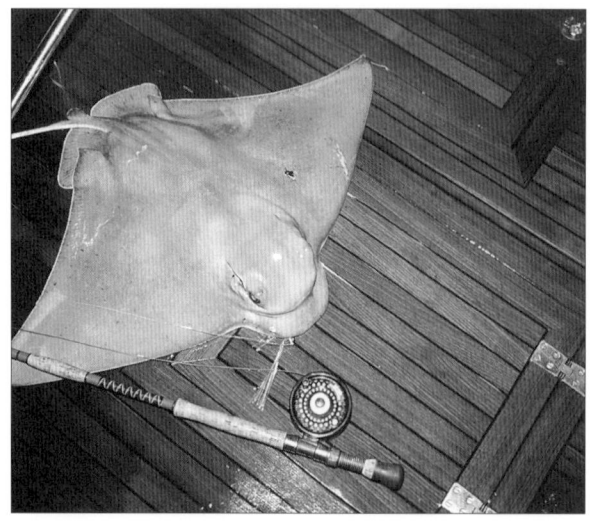

Even this hard-fighting eagle ray took a deeply sunken fly. You can catch almost every type of fish on fly!

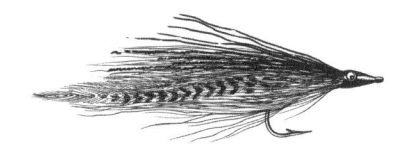

15
The game sharks – makos and blues

A metre under the inky blue surface I saw the take. The flash of ivory as the fly was intercepted was unmistakable. Sweeping the fly rod hard to the side, I set the hook. The rod tip jerked violently to disbelieving head shakes as the fish came to terms with the fact it was hooked. The spool of my big gold fly reel spun frantically as dacron backing sung over the guides.

Fifty, 100, 150 metres, then thirty kilos of blue and silver fish went ballistic, smashing violently through the surface, cartwheeling through the air and crashing back in an explosion of foam! Again and again it jumped, then the reel accelerated again! My god, we were still connected ...

There is a thrill about hooking a fish, any fish, on SWF. Following the exciting thump of the strike comes the sustained howling of dacron backing as it is dragged at high speed over the big stainless steel snake guides. The fight is the thing. Once the budding SWF angler has purchased some decent tackle, and worked through a few kahawai, mackerel and the like, thoughts may turn to the big ones. Unlike his or her freshwater counterpart, the saltwater fly rodder is not limited to one species.

In many areas, during the warm summer months, pelagic fish that are regularly encountered include blue and mako sharks. Porbeagle sharks may also be met with, particularly in the more southern waters of the country, and at least one has been taken on fly by angler Dave Carr. The commonly encountered smaller specimens (or 'rats' as gamefishermen term them), while beneath the notice of the big-fish addicts, are ideal fodder for the fly rod.

I have been fishing for sharks with flies since the late 1980s, starting in the bluewater off Hawke's Bay. Since then I have fly-rodded sharks in many parts of the country, including the Bay of Plenty, Northland and Auckland's west coast. These efforts have included three world-record captures, but initially I suffered a large number of lost opportunities until I worked out answers to many of the problems.

To bring the sharks within casting range is no real problem. A day drifting a likely area with a good berley trail running usually offers a reasonable number of chances to present a fly to a shark. In fact, the sharks often come up so close to the berley pot that you cannot show them the fly, and must wait until they move away from the boat a little. Casting ability is not really an issue with sharks.

The big problem is hanging onto the shark, once you have hooked it. By the regulations of the International Game Fish Association (IGFA), saltwater fly rodders are restricted to a 12-inch shock tippet. This may be wire, to offer protection from the fish's teeth. Catch 22 is that this shock tippet must be tied directly to the line class tippet – the monofilament leader that you are fishing. The IGFA recognises line weights of 1, 2, 3, 4, 6, 8, and 10-kg breaking strain for use with the fly rod. Most of the time, this monofilament leader comes in contact not with the teeth, but with the sandpaper-like skin, fins and tail of the shark, and is frequently damaged to the extent that it breaks. This used to result in the loss of around two out of three sharks I hooked.

You can, of course, use a longer wire leader if you just want the fun of playing the shark, but such captures are not recognised by gamefishing clubs or the IGFA for contests or records. Through long and sometimes bitter experience I have worked up a system that results in success about two-thirds of the time.

The secrets

My answers to the problem of leader damage are threefold. First, maximise the limited protection afforded by the shock leader and fly combination. I tie my shark flies on long-shanked hooks (or use tandem hooks) and use a figure eight round the hook stiff-wire connection to help hold the monofilament away from the shark's body. I also file the plating off the hook's point section, both to sharpen it and to promote rusting, so that any shark left with a fly will not keep it for too long (see the shark fly design in Chapter 5).

This fly-munching Hawke's Bay mako caught by the author illustrates the advantage of using long-shanked hooks for shark flies. At a whisker under 30 kg, it has stood as the 6-kg tippet world record for over a decade.

The game sharks – makos and blues

A small fly-caught mako has been tagged for release. The 30-cm shock tippet visible emphasises the vulnerability of the class tippet.

The second part of the recipe is to use hard leader material (see Chapter 2) that is resistant to the sandpaper skin of the shark. Also, keep your leaders short; work on the theory that the less leader you have, the less there is to get damaged. The minimum permissible class tippet length is 38.10 cm (15 ins) if you fish to IGFA regulation (see Chapter 6).

The final part of the mix is in the way in which you play your fish. In the early days we were reluctant to chase fish after they were hooked because it meant leaving a berley trail that we may have spent hours establishing, and if the fish was lost and the berley trail cut, you were left with nothing. However, playing the shark from a dead boat meant that the shark would often get considerable line out, which put a lot of water-drag pressure on the tippet. It also meant that the shark could get some very flat angles on the line, exposing the leader to constant rubbing from the rough body and tail.

A fly rod with a powerful butt action is needed to lift a stubborn shark.

95

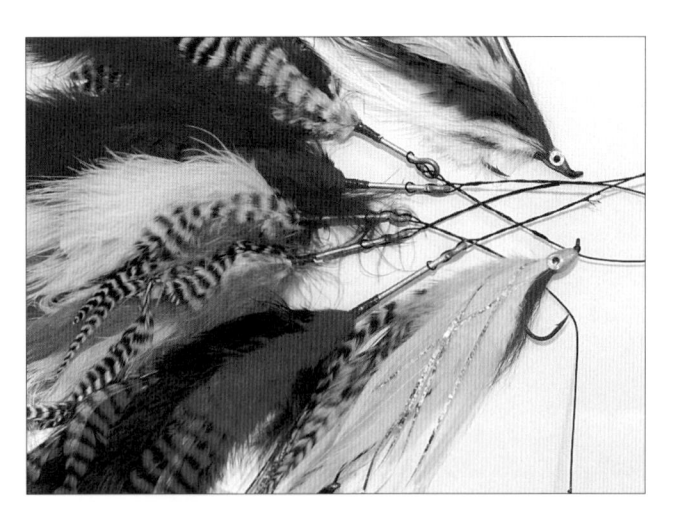

A bunch of shark flies with Lockweld shock tippets connected with a figure eight turn. The two on the right are tandem-hooked models by Pat Swift.

To have regular success, you must follow the shark with the boat. Stay close to it and keep the tippet off it as much as possible. This can mean some pretty nippy boat work, and having a switched-on helmsman is important.

But what of the berley trail? We found a way of having our cake and eating it too. By putting a big block of pre-minced berley in a plastic milk crate (to keep the sharks from gnawing on it), and attaching this to a large float, we could cast it off when we went off chasing a shark, and it would keep the berley trail going in our absence. A careful approach back to the crate after having finished with the first fish would often reveal more sharks in residence.

Presenting the fly

When sharks follow a berley trail to your boat, they are expecting to find something to feed on at the end of it. The odd one will take a chew on your boat, particularly any sacrificial anode that has an electrical field, such as those attached to outboard legs. Blues will generally vacuum up any moderate-sized pieces of berley, but unless makos have been conditioned by chunks in the trail, they often demand something of a reasonable size.

When light-tackle fishing for sharks with conventional gear I have found that even small makos will frequently refuse small strip baits, but will happily take a whole fillet of kahawai. When fishing for makos, the bulk of the fly can be important – more so than colour or pattern.

The shark takes your fly as just another piece of meat in the water. It is not important to retrieve it – letting it sit is usually the best way to go. The shark will often make a number of passes at the fly, increasing in regularity and proximity, before it takes. Be patient.

Sharks, when they arrive, are sometimes switched on and ready to feed, or maybe just mildly interested. This is more true of makos than blues. A 'hot' fish will move quickly and aggressively and will usually pounce on a fly as soon as it sees it. Other sharks may move more slowly, and appear to be disinterested in your presentation. These specimens may need some encouragement. Teasing them with a big bait on a rope – pulling it away from them, then letting them chew a little to get a taste – will often get them a bit more motivated.

Keep the fly up where you can see it, and once a shark takes, strike hard to the side so that hopefully you hook it in the corner of the jaw; this position will help protect the leader. It is hard to sink a hook point into tough shark skin with a fly rod, so a very sharp hook with cutting edges (not a round point) is a must, or you will drop a lot of fish. Strike as hard as you dare four or five times.

This Whakatane mako of just over 30 kg jumped over a dozen times and fought strongly. To a gamefisherman it would be a nuisance, but caught on fly rod it was for a time the world record on 10-kg tippet.

The fish

Among gamefishermen, makos, particularly big makos, are the most revered of sharks. They are immaculate blue and silver open-water hunters that can make some incredible jumps and don't take any nonsense from anyone or anything. There are numerous instances of makos, even quite small specimens, attacking boats after they have been hooked.

By comparison, in northern waters at least, the blue shark gets little respect as a fighter, is denigrated with the nickname of 'gumboot', and actively avoided by many gamefishermen. But since I began fly rodding for sharks, I have had to re-think my attitude to blues. While blue sharks may not give much of a fight on heavy tackle, they are honest fish on a fly rod.

You will sometimes hook a mako which refuses to fight, even when gaffed, but I have never hooked a blue on the long rod which didn't give powerful runs, and slug it out tenaciously. We once chased a blue, hooked on a 4-kg tippet, for twenty minutes, sometimes at near plane speed before losing it. While blues do not jump, they are more avid fly takers than their more stocky, powerful relatives, and often are more plentiful than the makos too. As a fly rodder, blues have earned my respect.

There must be good justification before any fish is deprived of its life, and this is

Lip-gaffed for release, Pat Swift (R) and Rick Wakelin bring a small blue shark aboard for unhooking off the Manukau bar.

something for each angler and their conscience to decide. Sharks are an important part of the food chain, slow to breed, and over-fished internationally. I can justify taking a very occasional shark for record purposes or a tournament if the fish is a real contender. Makos are a fine eating fish, especially if smoked. If the catch is eaten after the weighing and photos, I am quite happy. Otherwise there is the release option, with or without a tag. The good news is that sharks come close to the boat when attracted by berley, and may be closely evaluated before a fly is presented.

Ethics

Also down to the conscience of each angler is the ethics of the capture. Sharks, when hooked, sometimes seem to have considerable disbelief that something unfortunate like this could happen to them. Makos particularly will sometimes hang around the boat, shaking their head. If freespooled after the hook is set, they will also sometimes come straight back into the berley trail to feed again. Either way there is the opportunity for a 'cheap shot' with the gaff.

As a flying gaff may not be used, this is cheap for the angler, but not necessarily for the gaffer, trying to hang on to a 'green' shark with a fixed-head gaff. I do not consider it fair to gaff a shark before it has woken up and had a chance to fight, and have always refused such opportunities even on potential world-record fish, but I know there are one or two such captures in the record books.

The International Angling Rules state, in part: 'captures in which the fish has not fought or has not had a chance to fight do not reflect credit on the fisherman, and only the angler can properly evaluate the degree of achievement in establishing the record.'

At the gaff

If you have decided to take your shark, it must be remembered that to comply with IGFA regulations, a flying gaff may not be used. There are a number of specialised options in non-detachable head gaffs, most of which will need to be custom made. I favour a gaff with an overlong point, having had sharks thrash off a standard gaff. Gaffs with heads that rotate in the handle (but do not detach) help counter the rolling that is standard behaviour for sharks. The Australian-made Flexi Gaffs, with a very flexible fibreglass handle and a rotating head may be available in New Zealand by the time these words are published. Shark gaffs should have cutting edges on the point to aid penetration.

My practice, which has worked well to date, is to come in behind the leader and gaff over the top of the shark right in the middle of the gills. This seems to paralyse the shark briefly, and gives enough time to get a tail rope on before the fireworks start.

The ethics of keeping a shark should be considered. This 68-kg blue won the first Orvis SWF tournament and was an 8-kg tippet world record to boot, but the author is still in several minds if he should have kept it. At least you can smoke and eat makos ...

It has been suggested that a 'choker' noose would be a better way to deal with a shark than a gaff is, but again I think this would probably disqualify a fish (see 'acts that will disqualify a fish', numbers two and four in Chapter 6) under IGFA regulations.

If you are fishing for records or in a tournament, you must present your whole leader intact, along with an inch of fly line. Assuming you have made it that far, it is in the stoush at the gaff that the leader is often broken. If the angler is not involved in gaffing, then it is a good idea to take the pressure off the leader, and, using the rod, endeavour to keep the leader clear of the shark gaff handle, and other members of the crew.

As the record sizes for sharks creep up, the difficulty and danger of taking them on fixed-head gaffs increases. The heaviest mako (at the time of writing) taken on SWF is a 67.6-kg mako on 10-kg tippet taken by Kydd Pollock on Pat Langevad's 6.5-m boat *Fin* during the 1998 Orvis SWF Tournament at Tutukaka. Kydd fought the fish for forty-five

One of the controls on taking sharks on SWF is just how big a fish you can handle on a fixed-head gaff. Whakatane skipper Nigel Merry gaffs a record mako for the author. Photo: Pat Swift

The current (at time of writing) world-record 10-kg tippet mako is this 67-kg fish caught by Kydd Pollock (L), Petah Woollams and Pat Langevad off Tutukaka. Note the special swivel-head ladder gaff that Pat Langevad (R) is holding. Photo: Pat Langevad

minutes before Pat got a gaff shot. There was a fight on the gaff, which continued in the cockpit as the fish was brought aboard. At one stage it chased the third member of the team, Petah Woollams, out into the engine well, where a second mako was trying to eat the boat's propeller. Everyone had a few bruises to show, but the result was a great catch, doubling the weight of my own previous record.

It comes down to this: one man's meat is another's poison. While of little interest to gamefishermen, small to medium-sized pelagic sharks are powerful, exciting adversaries for the fly rodder. These sharks are available around most of our coastline during the summer, and if attracted by use of berley or chum, it is not difficult to present a fly to one. To those SWF anglers with access to a reasonable-sized boat, this is probably the easiest way to hook a big fish on fly. Catching it may be a different matter ...

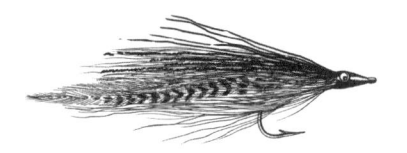

16
The small tuna

The small tuna species are great fly-rod opponents. Harder to get a fly to than, say, kahawai, they are also much more powerful fighters, and can just about set your reel alight on the first run. These powerful fish are very much the domain of the boat fisher, and are mostly found in offshore waters. Depending on the fish size and how game you are, tackle may range upward from 9 to 10 weight.

Skipjack and albacore are the main protagonists, and a third member of the mackerel and tuna family which regularly takes flies is the blue mackerel (also called slimy, English, and common mackerel). At much longer odds, but possible for the fly rodder, are frigate tuna, slender tuna, and butterfly tuna.

Skipjack tuna

Sometimes incorrectly called bonito, skipjack are often found in fast-moving surface schools, and I must admit to little success with the obvious method of chasing such schools with a boat and trying to cast to them. These fish often feed at such a pace that they are often gone in the time between when you begin your cast and the fly touches the water.

On the few occasions that I have got my fly in front of such skipjack, they have refused it, largely, I think, because standard retrieve techniques cannot get the fly moving fast enough for long enough to interest them. However, it is not impossible to catch skipjack with this method if you encounter them in the right mood and in sufficient density for the competitive spirit to motivate them into biting freely. On several occasions I have seen skipjack 'breezing' – feeding on tiny crustaceans on the surface in calm conditions, creating a surface ruffle similar to that created by a light wind. I have not had the

Probably the fastest light sportfish in New Zealand waters, skipjack can be hard to present a fly to, except when 'meatballing' or 'breezing'.

When the tuna are on the bite, wind and sea conditions hardly register on the mind any more.

opportunity to cast a fly to such fish, but it must be easier to get a presentation to them than those fast-moving skipjack feeding randomly on baitfish.

By far the most dependable way of catching skipjack on flies (no trolling, remember) is when these fish are 'meatballing' – herding up schools of small baitfish such as pilchards and anchovies and chasing them to the surface. Skipjack work well together, holding the bait and feeding in turn, at least until yellowfin, like the school bullies at a lolly scramble, crash the scene.

The meatballing scenario is most common in the Whakatane region in January to March. The best way for anglers to take advantage of it is to drift their boat close to a meatball that is under real pressure from predators. The bait will seek shelter under the hull and it is a big advantage to get a scoop or two of the baitfish as they go underneath. A relatively fine mesh net is needed for this. These baitfish are used as chum – both alive and dead – to keep the skipjack (and often albacore and yellowfin too) on heat as they circle the bait school sheltering under the boat like Indians around the wagon train.

Bigger skipjack are nicknamed 'water-melons' for their shape and stripes. This one took a surf candy fly off Whakatane.

In this situation, the skipjack are on tap, excitedly boiling on the chummed baitfish, and trying to attack the bait sheltering under the boat. This is a great fly-rod opportunity, and very exciting sight-fishing.

Sometimes the skipjack will hit anything. I well remember the first of these sessions on the *Pursuit,* a Whakatane charter boat skippered by Rick Pollock, who introduced me to this style of fishing. The wind was blowing 30 knots and conditions were pretty scruffy but the fishing was so hot that we hardly noticed. After an arm-stretching livebaiting session with yellowfin, I turned my attention to skipjack with the fly rod. The fly was riding like a kite in the strong wind, and after a fish or two hooked in the conventional fashion I found that by slowly lowering my rod tip I could have the fly dancing just above the surface, and skipjack were jumping 30 cm into the air to grab it!

Matching the size and colour of the baitfish that the tuna are on can be vital. Two useful patterns are (top) the surf candy and (bottom) a lightly dressed deceiver.

More regularly, however, you must do it right to hook even excited meatball fish on fly. This includes keeping the shock leader down in size (skipjack don't have big teeth, and 10 to 15-kg monofilament is plenty) or even tying the fly straight to the class tippet, having the right fly, and using the right retrieve.

If you do not have the right fly, you will soon know it – the skipjack that come racing in on the fly will turn off at the last moment. It may appear to the angler that the fish has just missed the fly, but if this happens several times you may be sure that it is a last-second refusal, and you probably need a different fly. I have found both colour and size to be important, and 'match the hatch' is the name of the game.

Try to match the size and colour of what the fish are feeding on. If the fish are refusing your fly, go smaller in size. Colour can also be important. Blue and silver or white has been very successful for me, and sometimes pink and white has worked well. A surf candy or sparsely dressed deceiver is my initial pattern of choice.

Retrieve speed can make a difference to the strike rate as well. These rapidly moving tuna are used to feeding at high speed, and will sometimes refuse flies that are moving too slow. In this situation, the only way to get the fly moving fast enough to satisfy the customers is to cast out, then move the fly quickly through the water with a wide sweep of the rod in combination with a long strip of the line made with your other hand.

This should allow a total of about 5 m of retrieve at high speed. If you do not get a strike in this distance, continue the sweep of the rod and throw a back cast, then shoot the line back out. This can become an almost continuous action, with the slapping down of the line and ripping it back off the surface serving to get the skipjack more and more excited until one takes. I sometimes use this same action to try and deliberately target the bigger fish, pulling the fly away from smaller specimens, but quick reflexes are required as you have only fractions of a second to assess the fish and react.

Once hooked, let the fish have its head initially – the first run is a howler! Once skipjack settle down, the fight consists of a lot of deep plugging and circling, but be prepared for the turbo charger to kick in at any time, especially when the fish first sights the boat towards the end. It's very exciting fishing!

Albacore

These fish are more 'user-friendly' tuna than skipjack. For a start, they are found over the full length of both our coasts, and are much easier to get a fly to than skipjack. Albacore are also to be found in a meatball situation, sometimes mixed with yellowfin and skipjack, although they can cope with much cooler water than their cousins.

Albacore can be located by trolling, and will often stay near a boat or hooked fish long enough to give a fly caster a chance. Using this method, troll a couple of favoured albacore lures, such as pink or zucchini hexheads or tuna clones. When fish are struck, work them in towards the boat as it slows to a stop and start throwing berley of chopped or whole pilchards over the side. With luck, the hooked albacore will bring their comrades with them, and the berley will hold them close to the boat. Here they are susceptible to cast and jigged lures – and flies.

This susceptibility to berley makes albacore much easier to catch on flies. I have pulled them out of berley trails run for sharks, and several times we have manufactured some

Albacore are a much more 'user-friendly' tuna than skipjack, and are easier to get a fly to. Photo: Rick Pollock

action by stopping in an area where a work-up has just died, and the birds that had been diving are just sitting around. Fifteen minutes of steady berleying with chopped pilchards has brought albacore up to the boat where they can be targeted. If you can get to a work-up while it is still active you may not need to berley to get your first hook-ups. This sort of activity is available in bluewater around much of the country at some stage of the season.

Again, baitfish imitations, like surf candies or deceivers, in the 80 to 100-mm range are a good starting point, and heavy shock leaders are not required.

Although albacore have much bigger eyes than skipjack, they do not seem to be leader-shy.

Albacore school and travel in a different form to skipjack: where skipjack spread out in a horizontal school, albacore school vertically. Partly, I think, because of this vertical schooling formation, I have had best results on deep-sinking fly lines.

Cast the fly and strip some extra line into the water to help the sink rate. Let the line get well down before beginning the retrieve. Be ready – it is not unusual for albacore to take flies as they sink.

Albacore will take flies at slower retrieve speeds than skipjack, but this still needs to be pretty fast! Maximum retrieve speed (that can be sustained for the full retrieve) is achieved by tucking the rod grip between your casting arm and body, then retrieve hand over hand, flat-stick, with the rod pointed down the line. When the take comes, keep pulling in line until everything is tight, and load the rod by swinging your whole body to the side. Hook-up!

You now need to concentrate on clearing the line that you have so recklessly stripped everywhere. Don't look up – concentrate on the snaking line, controlling it with one hand, making sure that you are not standing on it and that it is not tangled around anything.

One of the first albacore I hooked on fly was off Napier. All was going well until the last bit of shooting line lifted off the deck in a bunch. The tangle was small enough to run through the snake guides, but jammed at the rod tip. The knot broke with a crack, and I lost both fish and fly line!

Albacore are possibly not quite as tough and fast as skipjack, but still give a pretty respectable fight. I once spent 45 minutes on a 10-kg specimen using a 13-weight rod and 10-kg tippet.

Besides being a great sportfish for fly fishers, albacore are one of the best eating tuna species. If you intend to eat the fish, spike it in the top of the head, and bleed it by making a cut through the ridge about two finger widths behind the base of the pectoral fin.

The long shots

Other species of the mackerel-tuna family that fit the mould of this chapter are blue mackerel, slender tuna, frigate tuna, and butterfly tuna.

Of these four, only the *blue mackerel* (which, as mentioned earlier, is also known as common mackerel, slimy mackerel, frigate mackerel and English mackerel in various parts of the country) is regularly taken on fly. These fish are common in Northland down to Hawke's Bay, and straggle south to Kaikoura.

They may be caught in open water, and often school on the surface like trevally. They are keen takers of small to medium baitfish and shrimp imitations. We have taken them on fly in areas as diverse as Hawke's Bay, the Poor Knights Islands (before this area was closed to fishing, fly rodders could count on regular encounters with schools of these mackerel), and the Three Kings Islands. On conventional tackle, they have been caught in most places in between.

Blue mackerel grow to about 3 kg and put up a mercurial fight – very fast and powerful initially, but throwing in the towel after they have made a few runs. The larger specimens can be more dogged, and they are great fun on 7 to 8-weight gear. These fish make great cut baits but are not considered a great table fish in this country as they spoil very quickly.

Slender tuna grow to about 12 kg maximum, and are built as their name suggests: 6 – 8 kg is about average. Although they are reported occasionally from all around the country, the most reliable appearance seems to be off the east coast of the South Island, starting off Otago around Easter, and moving through to Kaikoura around May – June. They are sometimes encountered off Whakatane in spring.

Blue mackerel are another reasonably common fly-rod catch from the tuna/mackerel clan. Pat Swift pulled this one from a surface school at the Three Kings.

My experience of these fish has been off Dunedin with conventional spinning gear, although I believe the odd one has been taken on fly in this area too. They school on the surface, but the trick is to find some without a cordon of barracouta around them. Fast accurate casting would be required with a moderately weighted baitfish imitation such as those used on the other tuna species. The weight in the fly is so that it gets subsurface quickly – these fish don't hang around. They are real line-burners when hooked, and fight stubbornly. I suggest a 10-weight rod as a minimum if you intend to try and target these fish. They are not good eating.

Frigate tuna (not to be confused with frigate mackerel) are a small tuna of our northern waters. They look very similar to juvenile skipjack (the distinctive black belly stripes of the skipjack are not very obvious on juveniles), but can be distinguished by the big gap between first and second dorsal fins that skipjack do not have; 2 or 3 kg seems to be about as big as frigates go. I have occasionally encountered them in the far north in a hot summer. I have never heard of one being caught on a fly rod in our waters, but I believe they school and feed like skipjack, so one day someone may get a shot …

The final small tuna worth mentioning are juvenile *butterfly tuna*. Little is known about these strange-looking and enigmatic tuna. They have a head a little like a mahimahi, with large scales, and the adults (up to about 80 kg) are sometimes caught by offshore surface longliners. Schools of juveniles, whose huge pelvic fins give them their name (these fins stay the same size as the fish grows so are proportionately smaller on the adults) are sometimes encountered in the sounds and entrances of Fiordland.

Some years ago, Fiordland sportfishing pioneer Dick Marquand caught several on fly, and to the best of my knowledge is the only person to have done so. His technique was to drift down on surface schools marked by birds and leaping fish, and cast to them. Apparently they were not fussy about the type of fly, and fought well. Dick's comment was 'anyone could do it'. However, before you all go rushing off with your fly rods, I have fished the area on five or six occasions and have never seen a sign of one.

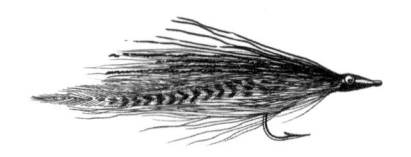

17
Yellowfin and mahimahi

Yellowfin tuna are a much-respected gamefish in New Zealand. They are seasonal visitors to our waters, the first of them normally showing up around early December, and lingering on until April – May. Hawke's Bay and Taranaki seems to be the limit of how far south they penetrate in any numbers, but the odd one has been taken off the southern Wairarapa coast, and I heard a report of one landed at Stewart Island during the exceptional La Nina season of 1998 – 99 – not unbelievable, as two striped marlin were caught off Haast that year.

At the time of writing, around twenty-five yellowfin have been taken on fly in New Zealand waters that I am aware of. All of these have been caught in the Bay of Plenty. Pioneering SWF angler Mike Godfrey caught three yellowfin in the early 1990s, and well-known writer and angler Mark Kitteridge caught the best to date – a 37-kg fish on a 10-kg tippet after a fight that lasted three and a quarter hours. This fish was accepted as the 10-kg SWF world record, and at the time of writing is the heaviest yellowfin taken anywhere in the world on fly under IGFA rules.

Quietly grafting away in this field is Opotiki guide Mark Draper, who without fanfare and with little recognition has engineered around 20 fly-rod yellowfin for his largely overseas clients.

Setting the scene

There are a number of scenarios that have proven successful when fishing fly for yellowfin. The obvious one – charging up to a school of tuna involved in demolishing a meatball of baitfish on the surface, and casting a fly into the melee – is difficult to achieve, and requires both split-second timing by the person on the helm, and rapid, pinpoint casting from the angler.

Getting on top of the meatball, as described in the last chapter, and letting the fly drift freely down to the tuna is a much more controllable situation, although you may have to work your way through a lot of skipjack and albacore to get to the yellowfin.

A third system has been developed from the observation of what happens when a boat moves off a meatball at the end of fishing. The yellowfin may have been hanging around the baitfish sheltering under the boat for some hours, encouraged to stay by the proximity of the meatball and the steady but moderate chumming of baitfish hopefully netted from the school as it went under the boat. When the boat moves off, the baitfish sheltering around the propeller become instant sashimi, others are disoriented by the turbulence, and suddenly the shelter of the hull has gone.

The effect of this on the yellowfin can be compared to a bunch of blokes who have spent a hot summer afternoon drinking cold beer and stoking the embers under a lamb-on-a-spit, constantly teased by the wafting odour of roasting meat. Finally the wires are cut, the spit is removed and the half-starved, half-cut mob are let loose on the tucker!

The yellowfin mass goes critical, and it is annihilation time on the defenceless bait, a few metres behind the stern! This is a similar situation to running up on feeding yellowfin, but is much more manageable. The boat runs off the bait and stops, the yellowfin go crazy, and the angler casts back to them. If there is no strike within a few casts, back the boat up to the remaining baitfish (who will be very glad to see you), change flies and repeat the exercise.

Finally, yellowfin can be attracted to the boat with berley of cubed pilchards or fillets of fish (usually skipjack), cut into cubes roughly 40-mm square, and fed

Mark Kitteridge took this 37-kg yellowfin off Whakatane on a cube fly after a three-and-a-quarter-hour fight. One of the great fly-rod captures, this fish became the world 10-kg tippet record, and, at the time of writing, was the heaviest yellowfin ever caught on fly. Photo: Mark Kitteridge

over the side, one at a time, in a constant trail. Flies designed to imitate the baitfish or cubes are free-drifted down the berley trail, where the tuna will hopefully take them.

Rigging for yellowfin

Yellowfin have about the best eyesight of any tuna, according to commercial research. The leader is important here. Firstly, it should be made fairly long (by saltwater standards): about 3 m between the fly line and the fly. Because the class tippet (maximum 10 kg if

Two types of fly are used for differing yellowfin scenarios. Top: a cube fly and a half pilchard fly (both by Pat Swift). Centre: a lightly dressed deceiver. Bottom: a pilchard tube fly (Pat Swift).

you fish to IGFA rules) is vulnerable to wear, it pays to keep this bit as short as possible – 38.10 cm (15 ins) – and make the extra length in the loop-to-loop butt section between the fly line and the class tippet (see the section on leaders in Chapter 3). This should be clear monofilament of 24 to 37-kg breaking strain.

Secondly, keep the thickness of the shock leader (the short section between the class tippet and the fly) down. I suggest 24-kg fluorocarbon, as it is less visible to fish than nylon, and very hard wearing. If using nylon, go no heavier than 37 kg for this section of the leader assembly.

Should you hook a reasonable-sized yellowfin, you may expect a fight that may go on for several hours with a lot of pressure being applied. Take particular care with all of the knots and connections; pay

American visitor Brian Horn took this 27-kg yellowfin tuna fly fishing a Bay of Plenty meatball with guide Mark Draper.
Photo: Mark Draper

attention to the strength of your fly hook; and be sure that reel, rod (and angler) are up to the pressure.

A reel with a spool machined from solid bar-stock (see Chapter 2), with a good drag and preferably anti-reverse handles, is the way to go, and you may like to consider a powerful fighting rod from either CD Rods or Kilwell with a harness lug that, in conjunction with a rod bucket, will allow the angler to give some rest to their arms.

After a yellowfin is hooked, it usually makes some long and powerful runs. Plenty of backing is needed and spectra or micro-dyneema braid is preferred as its fine-diameter-for-breaking-strain allows for a big line-load on the reel, and a reasonable strength without sacrificing spool capacity; 24 kg is suggested.

The boat may be used to contain the first runs, but the boatman should realise that fly reels with a 1:1 retrieve ratio do not offer a great line recovery rate, and must alter the boat speed to the angler's call.

When the fish settles, it is often into a dogged, plugging circle. You can try using the boat to change angles and break the fish out of its circle, but often it is a case of applying as much pressure as you dare, and being patient.

If you can catch a yellowfin on fly, you have really achieved something!

Mahimahi magic

For the fly rodder, mahimahi must be one of the most exciting fish to catch. These are open-ocean fish, but like kingfish they have an affinity for floating objects and respond to berley. While previously regarded as a tropical species, with increasingly warmer waters around New Zealand's coast, summer anglers are encountering them in the north on a more regular basis.

By trolling natural teasers (rigged whole fish or belly-flap strip baits) it is possible to bring them to the boat for a fly-rod shot, but the odds are pretty long against this in local waters. The best opportunity comes if you discover a floating object, such as a log, with a school of mahimahi in attendance.

I have not had the good fortune to encounter this situation in New Zealand waters, but have had a couple of good fly-rod sessions on mahimahi in Tongan waters. I am sure the same principles will work here in New Zealand.

The technique that has been effective for me in Tonga is to drift past a FAD or other floating structure, scraping flakes of flesh off a tuna frame into the water as the boat drifts along to create a berley trail. The mahimahi are not always right under the floating object, but may be hanging around within a couple of hundred metres. If the mahimahi are in a feeding mood (and this is not all the time), they will move into the berley trail behind the boat, where you can cast to them.

During a visit to Tonga for the 1999 International Billfish Tournament in Vava'u, our crew spent a couple of hours one day after the tournament targeting mahimahi on fly. We caught five and lost two: one pulled hook, and one when I ran over a line trying to turn the boat for a fish that had headed up around the bow, then doubled back, unseen.

Conditions were blustery, and the fish were really on the go, most of them 8 to 10-kg class fish. They showed a distinct preference for red and white flies, ignoring blue and white patterns. The fish gave magnificent performances, even on 10-kg tippets and 13-

weight rods. Each of them jumped ten to twenty times, often clearing the water by three metres, making screaming runs, taking hundreds of metres of backing, and finally, resisting doggedly. Fights lasted up to half an hour or more.

When mahimahi come to the boat, the colours are fantastic, and they are one of the best fish in the ocean on a plate – a wonderful all-round light tackle and fly-rod gamefish. I don't mind global warming if it brings more of these magnificent fish into our waters!

Acrobatic, powerful, pretty, and great on the plate, mahimahi are a great fly-rod fish. The author took this one in Tongan waters.

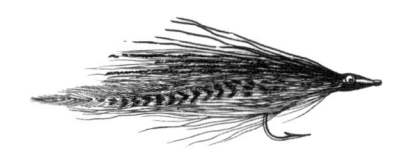

18
Marlin – the ultimate

Ten minutes from the end of my two-hour spell on strike, an angry marlin came up on the super plunger that we were using for a teaser. Deckie James Taylor teased the fish into the correct position in the third wake wave, as it slashed angrily with its bill at the plastic deception.

'Out!' came the call from skipper Bruce Martin up on the fly bridge of *Predator,* and I heard the engine note change as he pulled the engine out of gear. It all seemed like a slow-motion dream as I cast the huge fly across to where the teaser had been seconds before, then crossed to the port side of the boat so that the flashy creation would not get pulled into the now settling wake where the fish could not see it.

These are the longest seconds in fly fishing. Where was the fish? I had begun the third strip of the fly when I had an incredibly violent strike, which left a white line-burn scar right across my thumb. The marlin was on and running, but not for long. Abruptly, the leader parted and I was left with nothing but a limp line and shaking knees as the adrenaline backwash surged through my system.

We were all stunned. It was the first time we had attempted a marlin on fly and nobody had really expected to get that far. My two mates with still and video cameras had not even taken a shot. Wow! I sagged weakly down onto the fighting chair.

'Hey Bruce,' I said, 'I've got to do that again!'

To me, marlin have always been the ultimate gamefish: magnificent, powerful, fierce, a deep-ocean wanderer and apex predator. To catch one on a cast fly was for years a remote dream, and yet I had read overseas articles about catching billfish on fly off the Americas and Australia. It was an ambition I secretly nurtured. In those days many of my fishing acquaintances figured me to be a little crazy anyway, fishing at sea with a 'trout rod' – 'Hey mate, there's no trout here. Taupo's that way! Ha ha ha!! ...'

The billfish captures I had read of in overseas publications all seemed to be the lightweight sailfish, or juvenile marlin. In New Zealand our striped marlin (the smallest of our three species) average about 90 kg. In 1990, the largest marlin of any species ever caught legitimately on a fly, anywhere in the world, was 67 kg. I figured that some day I would have to travel overseas to somewhere that had a lot of small marlin or sailfish to achieve my ambition.

But the fishing gods move in mysterious ways. Things happened to bridge the gap between the inconceivable and the barely possible. The IGFA introduced a 10-kg tippet class, allowing a smidgen more firepower. I got a few marlin under the belt too, and started to lose my awe of them.

In the season of 1996, things crystallised. First, I had the opportunity of acting as second deckie for American SWF icon Billy Pate when he was in this country. I learned a lot from Billy, and ultimately saw him hook up on the only marlin we raised in five days, Secondly, whilst fishing at the Three Kings with skipper Bruce Martin on the charter boat *Predator*, I caught a 113-kg striped marlin on conventional 8-kg tackle after a six-and-a-half hour fight, a then world record. This showed me that I could catch a marlin on line this light.

Finally came word from Australia that my old mate Dean Butler had caught a 90-kg stripy on fly. It could be done! What I needed was the tackle and the opportunity. I had the chance, through Billy Pate, to purchase one of the fly reels that bear his name, and a month or two later it arrived by courier – big, magnificent, and smooth as silk. Then, a phone call came from skipper Bruce Martin: 'What do you reckon about having a shot at catching a marlin on fly at the Kings next year?' I literally could not believe my luck. A 'gun' skipper, boat and crew would be required to have any chance of success at a SWF billfish. A great many skippers would have treated such a suggestion with derision – a waste of time that would cost them fish off their season's tally – and yet here was one of the top billfish skippers actually keen on the idea!

It was too good a chance to miss, and May 1997 resulted in the experience at the start of this chapter.

The difficulties

As has been mentioned in earlier chapters of this book, the IGFA rules are not kind to those wishing

American SWF icon Billy Pate, in his trademark straw hat, ready for billfish action wide of Houhora. Pate was one of the pioneers of fly fishing for billfish, and the first to catch all species of marlin on fly.

to try and catch gamefish on regulation SWF tackle. The rules were drawn up many years ago, long before anyone thought of chasing big-game fish with a fly rod, but it is near impossible to change them now without devaluing the achievements of those who have gone before. If it was easy, the challenge would not be there.

There are three stipulations that have a major effect on catching marlin on fly tackle. First is the leader arrangement. Only 12 ins (30 cm) of heavy shock tippet is permitted. This shock tippet must be attached directly to the class tippet, which can be a maximum of 10-kg breaking strain. This means that the fish effectively cannot be traced and must be brought to gaff or tag on the rod. It also means that the leader is in constant danger of being damaged by the marlin's bill, fins, or tail.

Another rule, probably the essence of defining true SWF, says that the fly cannot be trolled, and that the boat must be out of gear when the delivery cast is made and during the retrieve. The effect of this is that a way had to be found to tease the fish up to the boat, where a fly could be cast to it.

'Bonze' Fleet (left) and Mike Brown with the fixed-head ladder gaffs used on marlin. Flying gaffs are not permitted under IGFA rules.

The final major difficulty is that flying gaffs are not permitted, so the gaffers have to hang on to a big, powerful fish with fixed-head gaffs should the decision be made to take the fish. This tends to limit the size of fish that can be handled.

All of this adds up to a tricky situation. You must first raise a fish, tease it up to within casting range, get it angry enough to take a fly, throw the boat out of gear, and cast the fly. If the marlin takes the fly, you must sink the hook with a fly rod into a bone-hard mouth. Then you come up against a delicately balanced equation: the increasing danger of damage to the poorly protected leader from a wood-rasp bill and lower jaw as time

One of Pat Swift's marlin flies, based on Bill and Kate Howe's 'flashy profile fly'. Note the two hooks. The 30-cm shock tippet gives an idea of the size.

moves on, added to the possibility of a tail wrap or the fish jumping and landing on the leader. The other side of the equation is that if you get an early shot and try and take a green fish with a fixed-head gaff, someone could get hurt, and the leader may be broken if there is a stoush at the boat, disqualifying the fish.

Tooling up

What we needed was Special Weapons And Tactics. Having spent four days on a boat with Billy Pate, I had learned a lot about his tackle and techniques. Armed with this and any information we could find in overseas publications, Bruce Martin went off to build a set of ladder gaffs: fixed-head gaffs with a handle section built like a ladder that, in the words of Billy Pate, 'you can really get your bones around'. I would sort out the tackle, leaders and flies.

I decided that I needed a rod with which I could really fight a big fish. It was to be a delivery tool to a teased-up fish, so it had only to throw a fly 15 or 20 m, but had to be able to really put some pressure on. Having spent five years professionally designing and building blanks and rods, I worked out what I wanted and went to local rod manufacturers CD Rods. The result is a 7 ft (2 m), moderately fast, two-piece taper rod, with full SIC guides (to combat wear from the spectra backing). I also had an over-large fighting grip made. They don't look as cool as a low-profile one, but I find that fatter grips are less apt to give hand cramps in a long fight.

The rod also had a small nylon gimbal nock under a butt cap, and a harness lug designed so that it will not tangle the shooting line. With this set-up, I could use a conventional harness and belt if I needed to rest my arms, or if the fish sounded and I needed to pump it back up. The finished product is now available commercially as CD Rods 'Downunder 14+'. It has taken a number of New Zealand and world-record fish now, including makos, yellowfin and marlin.

What I wanted in a marlin fly was the impression of bulk, without excessive casting weight. My first attempts looked like feather dusters. Rotorua-based Pat Swift would have to be the best tier of saltwater flies in the country, and sent me a couple of his creations to try, based on the 'flashy profile fly' designed by Americans Kate and Bill Howe, but modified a little. These are complex to construct, incorporating two hooks, and these days I source them from Pat – it is not as if I lose all that many of them. I carry about three basic colours and try to match them to the colour of teaser that is working best at the time.

Setting up the line

The line and leader knots and connections have to be of maximum strength to cope with the pressures involved, while trying to keep things relatively simple, and adaptable. The way I do it is described in Chapter 3, with some alterations to the fly line and leader section as follows.

Shooting line: this is 30 m of Cortland tubular weave nylon. Normally only available in 15 kg, the agents kindly got hold of some 24 kg for me. It is available in clear or yellow. Again, I used the yellow for visibility reasons. There is quite a bit of stretch in this section and it acts as a shock absorber, as well as a shooting line.

Fly line: the rod is rated at 14+, and I believe it is well in excess of this, maybe a 16-weight. Consequently I had to make my own fly line. I got hold of the heaviest line available, a Scientific Anglers 850-g Deepwater Express. After some experimentation, I cut a line that would cast like a bullet, and deliver a fly as big as a budgie. It is 4.80 m long, cut from the back end of the taper, with the thin end closest to the fly.

Leader butt: 24 or 37-kg monofilament with a loop-to-loop connection on each end.

Class leader or tippet: a hard leader type is critical, and the most difficult item to get hold of (see Chapter 2). Keep to just over the IGFA minimum length of 15 ins (38.10 cm), measured inside the connecting knots. The shorter the leader, the less chance of damage to it. Construction of the butt end of the class tippet is as described in Chapter 2. The tip, or fly end, of the leader is tied to a small solid brass ring with a uni knot tied in two thicknesses of line (the end doubled back). This is simple and easy, and, according to the knot testing work I have done, over 98% of the line's original strength. It also allows for accurate leader measurements and ease of changing class tippets.

Shock tippet: I used 200-lb Black Magic Hard Mono and crimp connections at each end – the fly at one end, and the solid brass ring at the other.

For those worried by the apparent complexity of this, or have trouble locating good leader material, Byford's pre-made leaders are available in this country, and have accounted for some very good fish without failure, including an estimated 75-kg marlin caught by Pat Swift after four hours and fifty minutes, and Mark Kitteridge's 37-kg yellowfin, which took three hours and fifteen minutes to land.

The fly gear ready to go, with a pre-measured length of line ready to be cast from the fish bin. Note the harness lug between the rod grips, and the specialist butt, designed to match with the 'Tri-Maxamizer' rod bucket.

Teasing

After much discussion between Bruce Martin and myself, here is the system we have adopted, based on overseas techniques. As I am a right hander, we pull up the right-hand outrigger (looking astern) so I can make my back cast out that side without tangling it around the outrigger. We run two teasers on 37-kg troll gear, and a daisy-chain teaser in short. The rod teasers are just lures that have been working well, with the hooks removed, rigged with 1-m leaders so they can be pulled out of the water easily.

The teaser on the left outrigger (looking astern) is run through a tightened-down roller troller. This teaser can then be pulled out of the water and left dangling from the outrigger when required. The other teaser, on the right, is run off the rod tip. Softhead lures are favoured for this work as they can be jerked into the cockpit without damaging boat, lure, or crew. The Moldcraft 'wide range' in various patterns is our benchmark teaser, with the angle-faced 'Bobby Brown' better in very calm conditions.

In recent times we have taken to running a third teaser from a reel clamped on the bridge rail out off the short outrigger position. The skipper can clear this one easily while also running the boat, and it allows a third colour combination to be run, increasing the chance of presenting the 'flavour of the day'.

Although they are popular overseas, I generally avoid natural teasers (sewn-up baitfish), although I sometimes use a heavily over-sewn belly flap inside a skirted lure, especially if the marlin are not attacking bare teasers enthusiastically. Our billfish are not spindle-billed sailfish or juvenile marlin from which teasers can easily be jerked away; they are big adult fish with very powerful jaws. A well-sewn belly flap will survive the attentions of most marlin, especially when partly protected by the lure skirt, but on two occasions I have had billfish break natural teasers in half and then swim off with 'their' half. Plastics may possibly be less effective at raising fish than a trolled baitfish, but we avoid the problem just mentioned. Keep it simple ...

The game plan is that when a marlin comes up on a teaser, the daisy-chain and bridge teaser (if used) are always cleared straight away. If the fish is on the daisy-chain or bridge teaser, it will nearly always drop back to one of the rod teasers after the former are pulled in. After the fish moves on to one rod teaser, the other can be pulled in.

We want to tease the fish up the left-hand side of the wake, so that the angler can cast to it from the right. (All of this is reversed if the angler is left-handed.) If the fish is on the right (short rod-tip) teaser, this means switching the fish across the wake. This should be done well back so that it doesn't lose the teaser in the white water of the wake. Whoever is handling this teaser rod just walks it across the transom, and the teaser and fish should follow. By now the other teasers should have been cleared away.

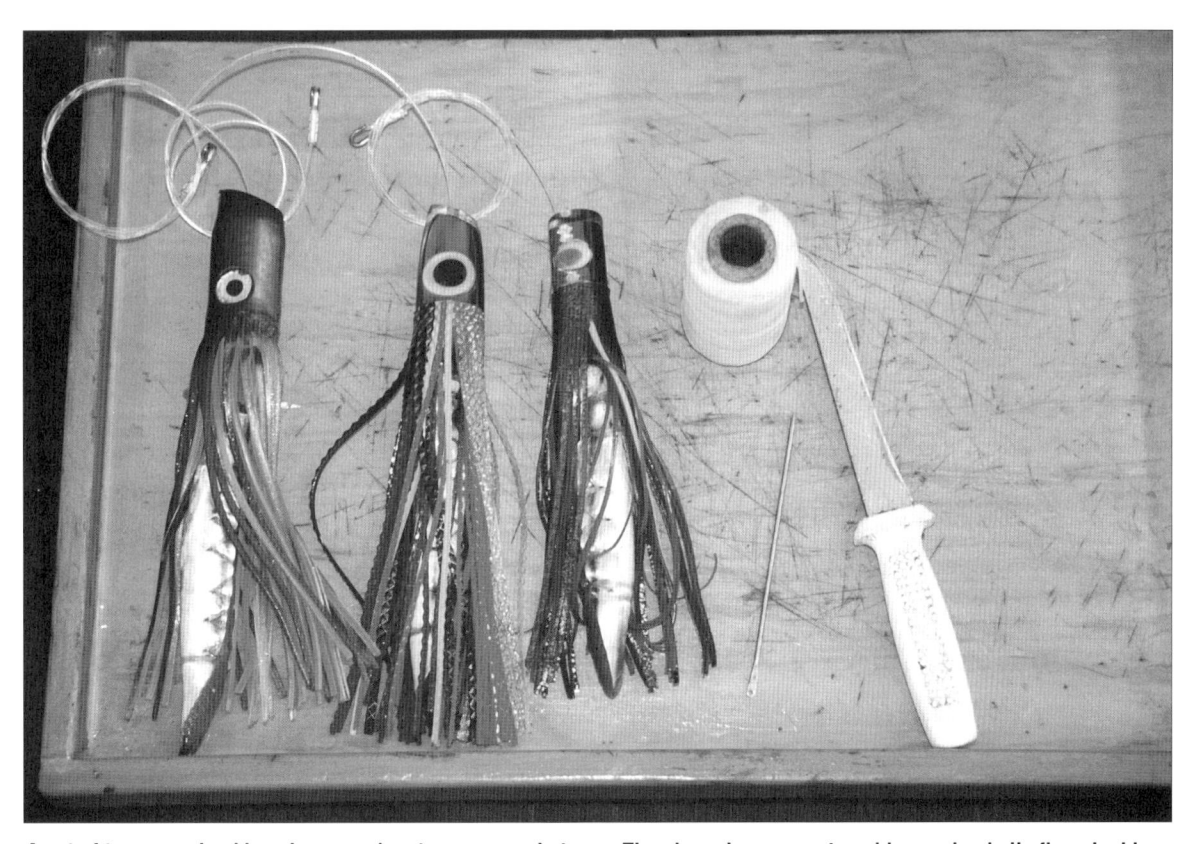

A set of teasers – hookless lures on 1-m traces – ready to go. They have been sweetened by sewing belly flaps inside to add flavour.

An angry striped marlin is teased toward the boat for a fly-rod shot. The teaser is visible on the surface ahead of it.

The trick of teasing is to keep pulling the teaser away from the fish, but not so far away from the fish that it loses sight of it. By the time the fish has been teased up to the boat, it should be fighting mad, and ready to attack anything in its path, including a fly.

When the fish is up at about the third wake wave, the skipper, who has the best overall vision up on the fly bridge, throws the engine out of gear, and shouts 'Out!' This is the signal that the boat is out of gear, for the teaser to be pulled away from the fish, and for the fly to be cast. Try to cast beside the fish, so that it sees the fly, but has to turn to take it. This increases the chance of getting a hook-up in the corner of the jaw, which is an easier spot to set the hook and helps protect the leader.

The first marlin

In the spring of 1997, I had a call from Bruce: 'I have a few days' gap in my bookings early in 1998. Come on up to the Bay of Islands and we'll have another crack at a marlin on fly.' Although I had some doubts about the numbers of fish at this time of year (in SWF you want 'lots of shots'), I was not about to pass up an offer like this, and Bruce was quietly confident.

The weather conditions were near-perfect. *Predator* was lightly loaded with water and fuel, and at her manoeuvrable best. By our third day of inactivity I was already thinking

Marlin – the ultimate

Boat trolling

Angler with fly rod

Daisy chain

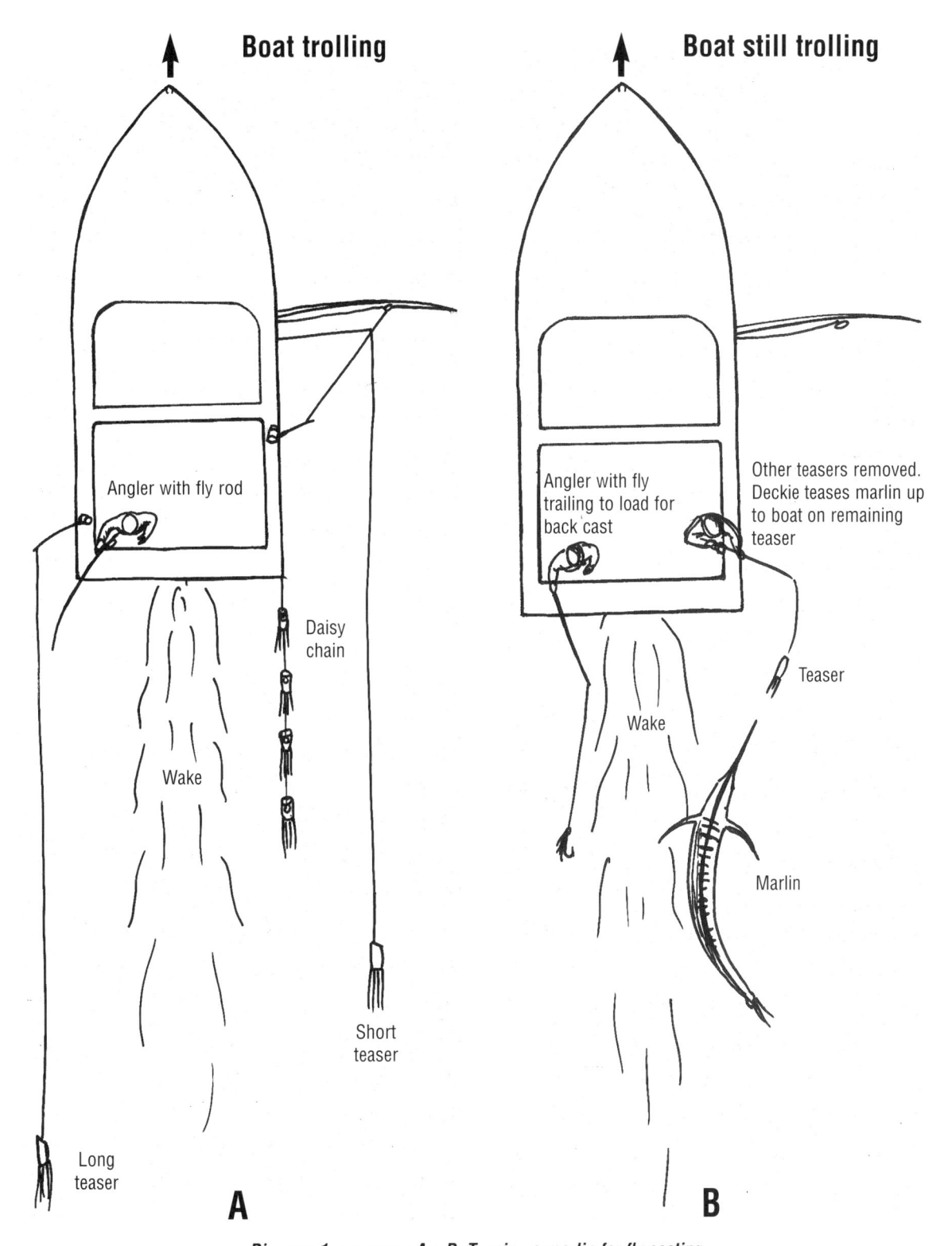

Wake

Short teaser

Long teaser

A

Boat still trolling

Angler with fly trailing to load for back cast

Other teasers removed. Deckie teases marlin up to boat on remaining teaser

Teaser

Wake

Marlin

B

Diagram 1, sequence A – D: Teasing a marlin for fly casting

121

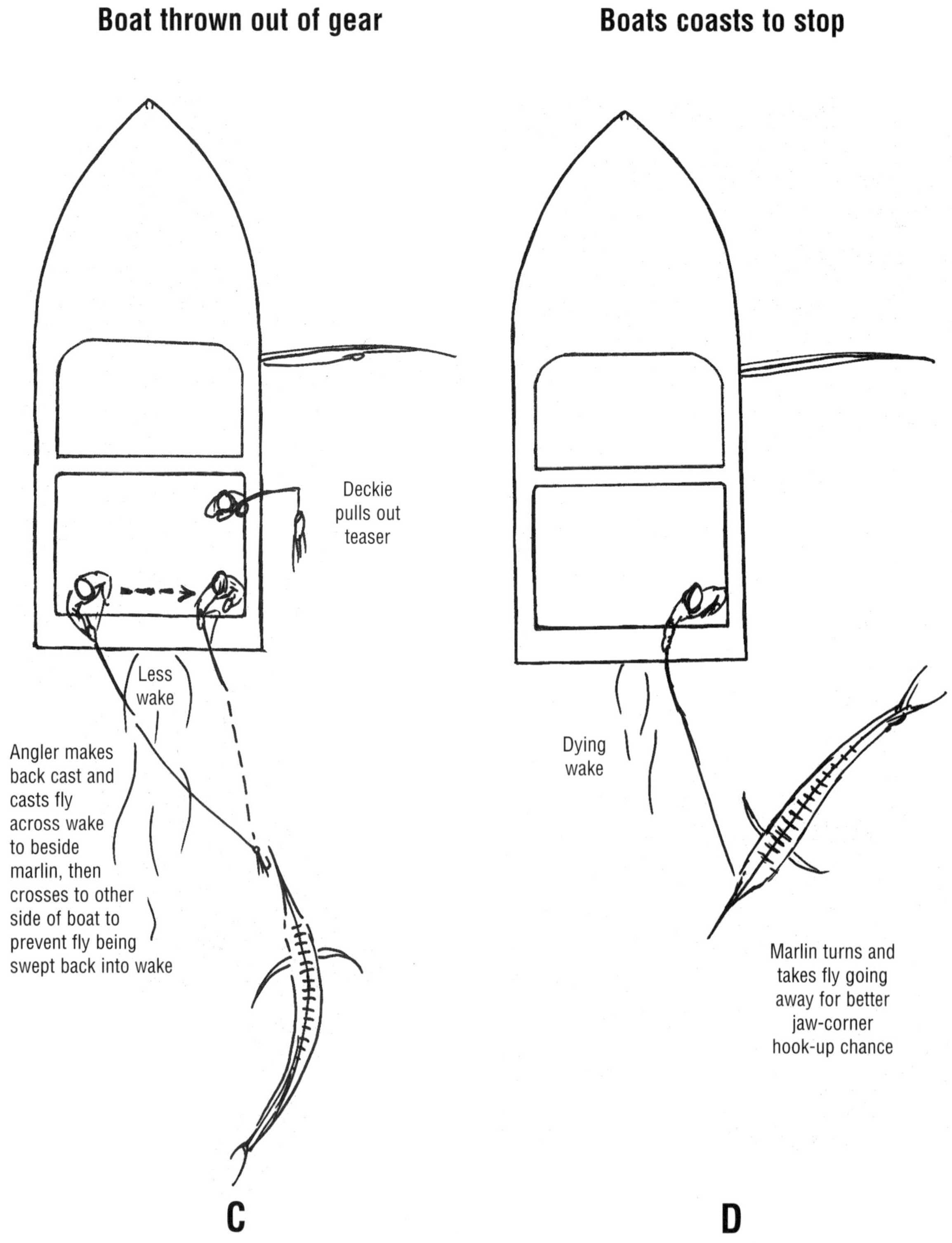

Saltwater Fly Fishing in New Zealand

Boat thrown out of gear

Deckie pulls out teaser

Less wake

Angler makes back cast and casts fly across wake to beside marlin, then crosses to other side of boat to prevent fly being swept back into wake

C

Boats coasts to stop

Dying wake

Marlin turns and takes fly going away for better jaw-corner hook-up chance

D

Diagram 1, sequence A – D: Teasing a marlin for fly casting

of trying again up at the Kings later in the season when there were more fish around. Suddenly everything changed. A black dorsal fin crashed across the daisy-chain teaser, ripping off the back two lures where they were joined with a parallel crimp, then vanished!

Suddenly the fish was back on the daisy chain. 'It's a marlin!' It vanished again, then crashed the blue-and-pink Moldcraft wide-range teaser.

Crewmen Mike Brown and Graeme 'Bonze' Fleet swung into action. Mike cleared the 'rigger teaser, and the daisy chain, while Bonze switched the fish across the back of the wake, and teased it up the left hand side. Dorsal up, the angry fish was right on the teaser, grabbing and striking at it.

'OUT!'

I cast – not my best effort, but close enough. Our fish was a magician – it had vanished again. I crossed to the left of the cockpit to keep the fly out of the white water of the dying wake as we drifted to a halt. Having done all this once before, there was no slow-motion unreality this time round. Where was it? As I searched the water behind the transom, the fish crashed my fly!

It was swinging its bill violently and seemed to have hooked itself on the strike. Although its head was facing toward me, and this is normally a no-no, I gave it a couple of good hits to make sure the hooks were home. The fish turned and raced away from us.

A fly-caught striped marlin comes up, head shaking.

New Zealand's first SWF-caught marlin, 84 kg on 10-kg tippet, caught in January 1998 by the author aboard *Predator* off the Bay of Islands. (L – R) The author, skipper Bruce Martin, deckie 'Bonze' Fleet. The other member of the team, Mike Brown, took the photo.

I let it take line on a moderate drag. It pulled about 300 m in a nice straight line, only making one porpoising jump. It settled down a little then, and Bruce moved the boat to contain it.

Over the next half hour the fish stayed near the surface, swimming steadily and making occasional sprints. Bruce manoeuvred *Predator* to keep behind the fish and keep the fragile leader away from its bill. The tackle felt great. The Pate reel had a good rate of retrieve for a 1:1 reel, and the CD rod had a nice sensitive tip, but plenty of grunt low down. I had a rod bucket on, but did not use it. A leather glove protected my hand from line cuts inflicted by the spectra backing. After half an hour, I really started to put some pressure on the fish, using my gloved hand on the line.

I found I could short-stroke in line, and move the fish across the transom. It made a short dive and came up with the fly line hooked under its tail. Again I put the pressure on, and suddenly we were going to get a shot at the tiring fish. It was right there! 'Take it Mike!' we called. It was a long stretch for husky Northland farmer Mike Brown, and he only made it with one hand, hitting the fish well back. It took off like a torpedo, ripping the gaff from his hand.

By good fortune there was enough buoyancy in the hollow aluminium pipe construction for the gaff to float, and we were able to retrieve it. Meanwhile, the fish was sounding. I put the brakes on to see what would happen. Under maximum pressure, the fish stopped, and using the power of the rod, I managed to pump it back to the surface. We had another gaff shot, and this time both Mike and Bonze got the hooks in. After a brief flurry, the fish was pulled through the transom door, and it was all over but for the gloating.

It took a while to sink in – New Zealand's first SWF marlin, caught IGFA legal, and the accomplishment of a decades-old dream for me. It had taken only forty-five minutes, or two years, depending on your point of view. On the scales it went to 84 kg (185 lb), missing the 10-kg tippet world record of the time by only 6 kg, but at that time possibly the second-heaviest stripy caught on SWF anywhere in the world.

This type of fishing is a true team effort: a skipper, angler and two crew are really required for best results. Everyone must play their part correctly or the whole enterprise comes to nothing. Without Bruce Martin's knowledge, enthusiasm and skilful boat handling, and the cool heads of Mike Brown and Bonze when under fire, none of this could have happened.

As Ernest Hemingway once wrote: 'The first is always the true record. Someone will always catch a bigger fish, but the first can never be caught again.'

Targeting marlin

A fly-rod marlin was also a personal ambition for Pat Swift, the Rotorua fly tier who had made the fly I had used. He suggested a five-day charter aimed exclusively at targeting marlin on fly, a thought that had passed through my mind too. Richard Dobbinson, who has represented New Zealand at the world freshwater fly-fishing championships, was our third angler. In early March 1999, we were on our way to the Three Kings on *Predator*.

On the second morning of our trip, we were on the King Bank. For the benefit of deckies Ant Loggie, Brendon Pearson, and anglers Pat and Dobbie, we had run a few drills based on what Bruce and I had already worked out – there are only two basic scenarios – and when a fish came up on the daisy chain we were all ready. I cleared the daisy chain and the fish dropped back onto one of the teasers.

It was a classic. The fish followed the teaser, slashing and batting at it, until it was about 10 m from the transom, by which time the other teaser was cleared. Bruce, with the best view of the fish from the fly bridge, made the call and threw the boat out of gear. Simultaneously, Brendon pulled the teaser into the boat, and Dobbie made his cast to the spot beside where the fish had been, quickly crossing the cockpit so that the fly would not get dragged across into the dying wake.

A few seconds of exquisite tension – where is he? will he take? – then the extremely pissed-off fish surged across the surface, head and shoulders out and pounced on the fly! Dobbie hit him as he powered away from the boat, but 50 m out, he came unstuck! The fly came back messed up. It was a hairy American pattern, and the consensus was that the dressing had been tangled around the rough bill of the marlin, rather than the hooks being in. This is not a problem with Pat Swift's much more sparsely dressed design, and he loaned one to Dobbie for any future shots.

The loss of this marlin did not seem to trouble Dobbie; he was stoked just to get connected – on fly – to the first marlin he had ever seen. I was relieved to see our first marlin of the trip, and that the boys had seen the system in action. When you organise these things, you feel a sense of responsibility to the party.

Pat was on strike next, and soon a double of beakies popped up on the teasers. One fish was teased in, but this time the switch did not go so smoothly; the fish over-ran the boat before it saw the fly, and disappeared. We quickly reset the gear, ran back over the area, and raised another single. This time, all went like clockwork. The fish nailed Pat's fly and hooked up!

This was a tough, stubborn fish. It worked slowly north during the fight, mostly staying

Angler Richard Dobbinson drops line to protect the leader as his marlin cuts up on the surface at the King Bank.

about 15 m down. Bruce and Pat tried lots of different angles, side-strain, and various manoeuvres, while staying behind the fish to keep the fragile 10-kg tippet away from the marlin's highly abrasive bill.

As the afternoon wore on, Ant and Brendan stood ready with the tag poles. We estimated the fish at 75 kg, and as this was not a record fish, Pat elected to release it – if we got the chance. Dobbie and I manned the cameras and waited for a photo opportunity.

Disaster! Suddenly the handle on Pat's fly reel came off in his hand! After all he had gone through to get the hook-up – the most important fish of his career – this sort of gear failure is infuriating. He almost threw it over the side in disgust, but controlled himself. Bruce used the boat to keep the tension on the fish, while we found Pat a screwdriver and he fixed the reel, then continued the fight, without anyone else having to touch the reel and so disqualify the fish.

Two things saved the day: one was that Pat was using an anti-reverse reel which allowed him to screw the handle onto a stationary handle bar even while the spool was unloading line; the other was that by this stage he was using a harness and a prototype fly-rod bucket developed by tackle designer Lewy McConnell, which we were testing, allowing him to free his hands to work on the reel.

Back to the fight. We found that if we stayed behind the fish and let it take up to 100 m of line, it would come to the surface jumping. After using this tactic four times, we could get closer to the fish. After about four and a half hours and twelve nautical miles, the fish broke back from its steady northerly course, and headed south. For the first time in the fight, the black shooting head came to the rod tip – we were only 8 m from the fish! It was right under the transom, but just too deep for the tag poles.

So close! Pat and Bruce had put on a flawless performance on the rod and the helm; everyone wanted this fish badly. Then, another chance – the tired fish was right behind the transom. A great underwater tag shot from Ant, and it was all over. After four hours and fifty minutes, an equally tired Pat deliberately popped the tippet and the fish swam free.

Pat was stoked – his first SWF marlin, and only the forth ever caught in New Zealand. (A further two had been tagged by American angler Tony Hedley fishing the Three Kings from Bruce Smith's *Striker* the previous year.) Our trip was a success already.

Pat had a lay-day on the following day, and picked a good time for it. It was overcast and drizzly, with 2 to 3-m seas on the King Bank. We persevered; a fish came up for Dobbie, but would not play the game. It had a look at the fly but would not take. Later in the day another fish showed briefly behind the back teaser, then turned away. Sea and wind conditions were getting very marginal for fly fishing, and the forecast was not great. We made the decision to run down to North Cape for the night.

A marlin on 8-kg tippet

By now, everyone had had a couple of shots but me, and I was starting to wonder if I would get a fly-rod opportunity before the end of the trip. I needn't have worried. The

Pat Swift battles a marlin using a prototype of tackle designer Lewy McConnell's Tri-Maxamizer belt. The Billy Pate Bluefin reel is unloading line fast! Nearly five hours later Pat tagged and released an estimated 75-kg striped marlin.

following day saw much better conditions and we worked the area off North Cape. Soon a fish popped up on the long teaser. Ant switched it across the wake and started to tease it up the left side, and I flipped my fly over the side in preparation for the cast.

Adversity! The wake sucked the fly down and it hooked up on the sacrificial anode! Bruce ran the boat ahead to keep the fish interested out the back, while I stripped the rod tip down to the fly and poked it loose. Whew!

Bruce slowed the boat and the marlin teased nicely. When it was on the spot, Bruce threw the boat out of gear, Ant pulled the teaser out, and I cast the fly. A flash of blue and silver and the fish surged half out of the water and nailed the fly! This has to be the biggest buzz in fly fishing!

It ran deeply astern, taking about 200 m, then came up jumping against a big belly in the line. The line went slack, and I wound in, expecting to see a broken tippet (I had gone down to 8-kg leader), but everything was intact – it had just thrown the hook.

Later in the day, I had another chance. I had just come on to strike, and was still organising my fly line when a fish popped up on the back teaser. By now the team were well drilled. When I cast my fly to the fish, it sat under it and eye-balled the flashabou and fish-hair creation. I gave a couple of short strips and the fish pounced like a cat on a mouse.

This was not a big fish – we estimated about 65 kg – but any fly-rod marlin is a good one. It would be a national record for the 8-kg tippet class if we took it, but I elected to tag. It ran off jumping, taking to the air about ten times, then sounded, before coming up and taking to the air again. I expected this acrobat to take apart my leader, but everything hung together.

Ready for release, a striped marlin and the fly that tempted it. Caught by Richard Dobbinson, it was estimated at 75 kg.

The good thing about all this jumping was that it tires the fish quickly, and it is less likely to sound. After thirty minutes it was jumping again, but we could see that it was tired. We came very close to getting a tag in, but not quite. By now I was pretty confident that I had the fish beaten, but you are never really sure what shape that fragile tippet is in.

The fish came up jumping yet again, but only getting half its body clear. As it shook its head towards me, I was forced to drop it slack line to avoid leader damage. It came close to the transom and Ant made a perfect mid-air tag shot on the exhausted fish.

Great stuff! I had come on this trip with the idea that it would be a success if we caught one marlin on fly, but here was a second. The whole procedure, which had seemed to be fantasy fishing when we had first tried it three seasons before, now almost seemed commonplace.

The statistics for the trip: we raised nine marlin, cast to six, hooked four, and tagged two – the fourth and fifth SWF marlin caught in New Zealand. A subsequent trip a year later, with the fish not quite so co-operative, saw sixteen marlin raised in five days, four hooked and one tagged by Richard Dobbinson. With the right tackle and technique, catching marlin on SWF is quite an achievable thing – you just have to concentrate on it!

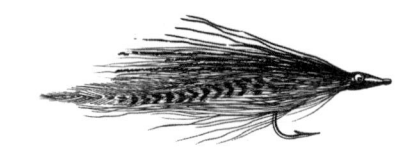

19
Sweet water and salt

Like many fishermen, I have a little photo album of special fish. These are not always the biggest or record fish, but just catches that have meant something special to me for the place, the people or the circumstances of the catch. I was having a bit of a flick through it the other day, and a thing that struck me was the high proportion of fly-rod-caught fish, highlighting the big enjoyment and satisfaction aspects of saltwater fly fishing.

I guess you could call me (among other things) a bit of a fly-rod nut. I spent a lot of years waving the long wand for trout the length and breadth of both islands of this country, including three years living on the banks of the Tongariro river. Although many fishing writers like to portray saltwater fly fishing as merely an extension of the freshwater branch of the sport, on reflection I feel that there really are some fundamental differences in attitude and approach which set the two apart.

On the sweet water, a great deal of the pleasure is found in just being there – the musical run of the waters, the trees and wildlife changing through their seasons, the pleasure of laying out a near-perfect cast that tugs an inch of line from the reel, proving that you could have cast further if you had wanted to. And there is always the hope that, just around the next bend, there will be that special, deep, almost mystical pool that might hold the big one.

Saltwater fly fishing, on the other hand, is as much about the fish as the environs. Although oceanic wildlife, and the sea itself, hold a deep fascination, any sort of marine fishing will provide opportunities for these encounters. Using fly gear at sea is considerably more of a challenge than working with bait or lure on standard tackle.

I still enjoy the odd trout fish, mostly for the pleasure of being in the places where trout are found, and for the joy of fooling the trout into accepting an artificial fly. For me, once the hook goes in, the rest is a bit anticlimactic. I have been spoiled by fly fishing at sea. The raw power of saltwater fish makes a trout look pretty tame in that department.

Trout are the main target of the freshwater fly fisher. In general they are usually browns or rainbows between 1 and 4 kg in weight. A comparative saltwater fish, the kahawai, grows to a similar size but has many times the power of a trout – ask anyone who has caught both on similar fly tackle.

This is all a matter of evolution and environment. A feeding trout does not have to work too hard, and when under threat has only to dash as far as the nearest snag or deep hole. The feeding and defence of a fish like a kahawai rests on it being able to swim faster than its prey, and anything that, in turn, wants to eat it.

But SWF does not stop at kahawai. Trevally, mackerel, snapper and a wealth of inshore bottom fish may all be caught on fly. Inspired anglers lift their sights to the brutal kingfish, and the high-speed oceanic fish like skipjack tuna, albacore or yellowfin tuna. There are sharks of all species and sizes, and even the ultimate – a marlin on saltwater fly! There is almost no limit to the size or species of saltwater fish that may be encountered. In the last couple of years several small broadbill swordfish have been caught on fly off the African coast.

I don't fly fish all the time, of course. Often the technique is plain impractical for the situation I am in, for one reason or another. I also believe that variety is the spice of life when it comes to fishing. Different species, different places and different techniques all help keep the game of fishing interesting, but there is a mystique about fishing fly that keeps me coming back to the long rod more and more.

I have had my comeuppance a few times with some big fish, and in particular remember an unknown beast that really wiped my nose at Cape Runaway over a decade ago. The fish took a six-inch deceiver fished deep in the berley trail and lived up to the name of the area. The pitch of the reel screamed higher and higher as the decreasing spool diameter forced it to spin faster and faster. In one high-speed sprint, without deviation or pause, it had the big Fin-Nor fly reel two-thirds empty. Over 250 m of line were out before water pressure popped the tippet. It took five minutes to wind the line back on the reel afterward! All these years later, I still wonder what that fish was ...

Glossary

Anti-reverse – a reel on which the handle remains stationary when line is running out.
Aquaseal – a type of wader repair glue often used for securing joins and splices on lines.
Arbour – the central support pillar of a reel spool.

Back cast – the section of a fly cast where the line is thrown behind the caster.
Backing – reserve line for playing a fish that pulls out all the casting line.
Backwash – where the sea working in and out of a rock gully causes a turbulent area.
Balanced rig – a rod, reel and line unit that works in harmony.
Belly flap – the belly portion, usually of a small tuna, sewn up to make a bait.
Berley – ground bait or chum; a preparation used to attract fish, which usually includes minced fish.
Berley pot – a tube with holes drilled in it, used to dispense berley.
Bite leader – see shock tippet.
Blank – the bare fibreglass or graphite tube on which a fishing rod is built.
Braided mono – a hollow line made by weaving fine monofilament in a tubular fashion.
Braided mono loop – a fly line end loop spliced from a section of braided monofilament.
Bridge teaser – a teaser that is run and controlled from the fly bridge of a launch.
Broken water – a patch of sea that is breaking or rough.
Bucktail – the hair from the tail of a deer used to tie flies; also a fly made from this material.
Bury – when line under pressure digs into and jams in loosely wound line on the reel.
Butt – The end section of a rod below the reel seat.

Ceramic (guide) – a type of line guide on a rod that has a metal frame and ceramic ring.
Channel marker buoy – anchored buoy that marks a shipping channel.
Choke point – a geographic structure where a waterway (and fish) runs through a narrow gap.
Choker – a rope, wire or chain noose placed around the head of a shark to secure it.
Choking – when a thick line runs through a narrow line guide with excess friction.
Chum – see berley.
Class tippet/leader – that section of a (usually) monofilament fly leader that defines its breaking strain.
Cod pot – a cage-style fish trap used for catching blue cod.
Componentry – the accessories (reel seat, guides, etc.) that are used to build a fishing rod on a blank.
Cork composite drag – a drag on a fishing reel that has soft washers formed from re-processed cork.
Countdown – a method of estimating depth by slowly counting as the line sinks.
Counterbalance – a weight set opposite the handle on a reel to ensure it spins smoothly.
Crimp – a metal sleeve used when rigging monofilament or cable.
Crustacean – a member of the family Crustacea, which includes crabs, shrimps and crayfish.
Cubes – pieces of fish cut into rough cubes.
Cubing – attracting fish by berleying with cubes.

Dacron – a woven synthetic fibre often used as fly-line backing or gamefishing line.
Daisy chain – a series of lures rigged spaced apart on a single trace, often used as a teaser.
Dead-drifting – a way of fishing a fly by letting it drift without retrieving it.
Delivery cast – the final cast which delivers the fly to the water or fish.
Dorsal (fin) – the fin on the top of the back of a fish or sea mammal.
Double haul – a double sequence of hauling the line during the cast to increase line speed.

Glossary

Drag setting – the amount of drag on the line as a fish pulls it from the reel.
Drop back – in this case, the act of dropping back a fly and letting it sink again after a partial retrieve.
Dry fly – in freshwater fly fishing, a fly designed to float on the water surface.
Dumb-bell eyes – a pair of metal eyes used in tying flies, connected by a bar of the same material.

Eel grass – a type of grass-like marine weed usually found in shallow estuaries.
Exposed spool rim – an aspect of reel design where the spool rim is wrapped over the outside of the frame.
Extension butt – on fly rods, an extra section that can be added to the butt to increase the length.

FAD – Fish Aggregation Device; usually an anchored buoy, chain and rope, used to attract pelagic fish.
False casting – a series of casts made to work line out of the rod, rather than deliver the fly.
Ferrule – a joint in a rod that allows disassembly for ease of transport and storage.
Fighting grip – on a fly rod, an extra grip above the casting grip to increase leverage when fighting a fish.
Filamentous algae – a green hair-like weed found in estuaries and harbours.
Fixed handle – a reel handle fixed to the spool which spins with the spool.
Fixed-head gaff – a gaff that has the head permanently attached to the handle.
Flats fishing – casting to (usually) visible fish in extensive shallow-water areas.
Fluorocarbon – a type of monofilament line that is harder and less visible in the water than nylon.
Flying gaff – this gaff has a rope attached to the head, which detaches from the handle after a fish is struck.
Fly line – a line especially for fly casting; usually has a plastic coating over a braided core.
Forward cast – that portion of a cast where the line is propelled forward of the caster.
Fusion line – a type of polyethylene line where the fibres are fused together rather than braided.

Gimbal nock – a slotted cap on a rod but made to fit into a pin in a rod bucket.
Gravid – a fish with fully ripe gonads that is ready to breed; pregnant.
Gutter – a trench of deeper water off a beach, running parallel to the shore.

Handlining – pulling in a fish on a line without use of a rod and/or reel.
Harness lug – a lug on a rod or reel that a clip attached to a harness may be attached to.
Haul – pulling on the fly line during a cast to increase line speed.
Hexhead – a type of skirted troll lure with a head of chromed hexagonal brass.
Hua – the gut portion of a paua (abalone).

IGFA – the International Game Fish Association; it keeps the world-record lists and governs fishing rules.

Jig – a (usually) metal lure that imitates a baitfish.
Jigging – fishing a jig in the vertical rather than horizontal plane.
Junction – a spot where two or more channels meet.

Krill – a small red-coloured crustacean fed on by many fish, birds and marine mammals.
Krilling – fish surface-feeding on true krill or other small crustaceans and larval fish.

Ladder gaff – a fixed-head gaff with a branching handle joined by crossbars in ladder fashion.
Large arbour reel – a fly-reel design that has a large-diameter centre to the spool.
Larval baitfish – any small fish in its larval stage, resembling whitebait.
Leader/tippet/trace – the section of (usually) monofilament joining fly line and fly.
Line recovery rate – the speed at which line can be wound back onto a reel.
Line weight – an arbitrary numerical rating system allowing fly rods to be matched to suitable fly lines.

Lockweld/Twistweld wire – a plastic-coated wire cable joined by twisting together then melting the plastic.
Loop-to-loop connection – where two lines are linked by passing end loops through and over each other.

Marabou – a soft fluffy feather from the marabou stork used for fly tying.
Meatball – a tight school of baitfish herded up by predators.
Micro-dyneema – an advanced low-stretch synthetic line used as backing on fly reels.
Multi-washer drag – a reel drag system made of a sequence of hard and soft washers.

Nymph – in fresh water, the larval stage of an aquatic insect or an artificial fly that imitates one.

Outrigger – a long pole mounted on a boat that trolls a bait or lure away from the side of the boat.
Over-line – use a heavier line on a fly rod than its rated weight.

Packing – line wound on a reel with the aim of increasing the arbour diameter.
Palmer style hackle – a feather wound in a spiral along a hook, giving a bottlebrush effect.
Pelagic – fish that inhabit and feed in mid to surface waters; often migratory.
Piscivorous – any creature that eats fish.
Polyethylene – a plastic used to manufacture thin, very low-stretch lines used for fly-line backing.
Popper fly – a fly designed to splash on the surface, imitating fleeing or injured baitfish.
Popper head – a separate head that can be added to a standard fly to make it pop on the surface.
Presentation – the manner in which a fly is exhibited to a fish.
Pump – a way of fighting a fish by lifting it with the rod, then winding in the line as the rod is lowered.
Purse-seiner – a commercial fishing boat that encircles school fish with a net, then closes it by drawstring.

Rat – a small specimen of a gamefish, particularly kingfish or mako shark.
Reel capacity – see spool capacity.
Reel seat – the fitting on a rod in which the reel is mounted.
Refusal – when a fish inspects but will not take a fly.
Retrieve – to make a fly 'swim' by pulling in the line.
Retrieve speed – the speed at which a fly is retrieved.
Reverse tie – a fly designed to swim point up.
Roller troller – a release clip where the line runs around a hinged roller that pops open when pulled hard.

Sabiki – a string of flies tied on branch lines off a main trace, often used to catch baitfish.
Sacrificial anode – usually a sacrificial zinc block on a boat or engine to prevent corrosion.
Schooling – fish swimming and/or feeding in a group, usually on the surface.
Sea lettuce – a type of green lettuce-like weed that grows on open sea coasts.
Selective feeding – when a fish will feed exclusively on one prey item.
Shock tippet (also bite leader) – a section of heavier line or wire that protects the class tippet from the fish.
Shooting basket/bucket – a container strapped around an angler's waist into which the fly line is stripped.
Shooting head – a short, heavy fly line that tows out a lighter shooting line when cast.
Shooting line – see shooting head.
Shooting the line – the act of letting line run through the rod guides when casting.
Short outrigger position – a spot partway along an outrigger where a second line can be run.
SIC guides – top-quality rod guides with silicon-carbide ceramic rings.
Sight fishing – casting directly to sighted fish.

Single action reel – a reel that gains one turn of the spool for one turn of the handle.
Sink rate – the speed at which a line or fly sinks through the water.
Sink time – the length of time it takes for a fly or fly line to sink to a certain depth.
Skirted lure – a troll lure with a skirt of split plastic, fabric, feathers or similar material.
Smelt – a small freshwater baitfish often fed on by trout.
Snake guide – a simple wire line guide used on fly rods.
Softhead lure – a skirted trolling lure with a soft plastic head, often used as a teaser.
Sonic tag – a sonic tracking device attached to a fish for research purposes.
Sound – when a hooked fish runs straight down into deep water.
Sounder – a SONAR device used to show fish and bottom structure on a screen.
Spectra – a type of thin, low-stretch, braided polyethylene line, often used as fly-line backing.
Spool capacity (also reel capacity) – the amount (length) of line that a reel spool can carry.
Standing line – when making knots, the main body of the line (see tag end).
Straylined bait – a bait drifted down through the water column with little or no added weight.
Streamer – a general fly type, designed to imitate a baitfish.
Strike indicator – any coloured or small floating object attached to the line to help indicate a strike.
Strike zone – the area of water where fish are found or strikes are regularly happening.
Stripping guide – the first and largest line guide at the bottom of a rod.
Strip retrieve – to retrieve line by pulling it in by hand in short lengths.
Structure – a formation of any type which may provide food or habitat and attract fish.
Superbraid – a thin low-stretch line made of braided polyethylene, used as fly-line backing.
Super plunger – a large Hawaiian skirted lure, sometimes used as a teaser.

Tag – a numbered piece of plastic-covered wire attached to a fish for research purposes.
Tagging – attaching a tag to a fish with a small stainless dart.
Tag end – the short, loose end of a line used when knotting (see standing end).
Tag shot – making the attempt to tag a fish with a tag mounted on the end of a pole.
Tandem-hook fly – a fly made with two single hooks.
Taper (line) – the shape and structure of a fly line, regarding thickness and length.
Teaser – a hookless lure or natural bait trolled to attract gamefish.
Teasing – the act of using a teaser.
Tippet – see leader.
Top shot – a shorter length of functional line, with a packing line under it.
Trace – see leader.
Tube fly – a fly constructed on a hollow tube; the hook/leader runs up the inside of the tube.
Tuna clone – a type of skirted troll lure used for tuna.
Twistweld wire – see lockweld.

Wake waves – the pattern of waves created by a moving boat, used to describe position (for example: third wave back).
Water column – the sea regarded as a cross-section from seabed to surface.
Weight forward – a type of fly line where most of the weight is at the front (see taper).
Wet fly – a fly designed to be fished beneath the surface; usually small freshwater types.
Work up – an area of activity where fish, birds and other predators are attacking baitfish.

Zucchini – a popular lure colour consisting of lime-green, orange and yellow.

Index

albacore 104-105

backing 25-27
barracouta 14, 81-82
berley 13, 14, 53, 60, 64-65, 68, 75, 84, 89, 96, 111
berley fly 44

casting 33-38
chokers 99
Clousers minnow 13, 41, 68-69, 74, 82, 89
cod, blue 89-92

dacron 19, 24, 25
deep-water techniques 11, 65-66, 69, 70-71, 88-92
double haul 36-37

estuary fishing 10, 57, 66

FAD 76-78
false casting 35
flashy profile fly 117
flatfish 86-87
flies 39-46, 48
flylines 20-22, 27-29, 47, 117
fly tying 39-46

gaff, fixed head 49, 51, 99, 115
gaff, flying 49, 51, 115
goatfish 52
gurnard 85

hapuku 88-91
hapuku, granddaddy 52
hooks 13, 39-46, 48, 53, 94

IGFA regulations 30-31, 47-51, 74, 94, 95, 99, 114-115

jock stewart 52, 56
john dory 85-86

kahawai 13, 57-60
kingfish 73-78
koheru 52, 53

leaders 12, 22, 29-32, 48, 57-58, 95, 109-110, 115, 117
Lefty's deceiver 13, 41-42, 74, 103, 105
loading the rod 35

mackerel, blue 106
mackerel, jack 14, 52-54

maomao 52-54, 92
mahimahi 111-112
marlin, striped 10, 113-129
meatballs 102-103, 108-109
mullet, yellow-eyed 52, 53

packing 23-24
parore 83-84
perch, butterfly 52, 56
piper 52, 53
popper heads 45-46, 74
popper flies 45

ray, eagle 92
reefs, inshore 11
reels, fly 15, 17-20, 23, 48, 111
rods, fly 16-17, 48, 116-117

salmon 10
scarpies 56
shark fly 43-44, 96
sharks 11, 93-100
shark, blue 97
shark, mako 97
shooting basket 37, 38
shooting head 27-28, 37
shooting line 27-28, 37, 117
shore fishing 11, 57-59, 66
snapper 67-72
snapper, golden 92
stargazer, spotted 52, 56
superbraid backing 19-20, 25-27
super shrimp 44-45
surface schools 11, 59-60, 61-64, 75, 78
surf candy 42-43, 103, 105

tarakihi 87
teasers 111, 113, 118-120, 121-122
trevally 61-66,
trumpeter 56, 90-91
tuna 11, 101-107, 108-111
tuna, butterfly 107
tuna, frigate 107
tuna, skipjack 101-104
tuna, slender 106-107
tuna, yellowfin 108-111

warehou 79-81
wire shock leaders 14, 81-82, 94
wrasses 52-56, 91